OLD WORKINGS

OLD WORKINGS

Gordon Hodgeon

mudfog

First published 2013
by Mudfog Press
c/o Arts and Events, Culture and Tourism,
P.O. Box 99A, Civic Centre, Middlesbrough, TS1 2QQ
www.mudfog.co.uk

Cover Design by turnbull.fineart@btinternet.com

Print by EPW Print & Design Ltd.

ISBN: 978-1-899503-06-3

Mudfog Press gratefully acknowledges
the support of Arts Council England.

ARTS COUNCIL ENGLAND

Middlesbrough
moving forward

This book is dedicated to

Julia

and to our children

and grandchildren

My thanks are due to Andy Croft and to several of my carers, who have helped me put this selection together and do all the necessary editorial work in preparing for publication.

Contents

Uncollected Poem

From *Winter Breaks* 2006

***Winter Breaks* - poems from the sequence**

Uncollected Poem

From *Still Life* 2012

Uncollected Poem

New Uncollected Poems 2013

Uncollected Poems

An Old Walk
Leigh, Lancashire

I walked down the cinder road
from the old railway bridge.
The track beneath is empty, rails torn up
and the bridge lies bent, a low black beast,
on which the carlights slide up, down
the line of bone, the skyback
split to its spine, flanks cut away;
its reason gone with the last train
it still crouches, hoarding nothing.
I look over the wide flash, the bright water
holding the little light,
cross the broken fence and stand, trying to see.
The council tip holds in the flash this side
from the road it used to flood.
Sodden papers, bike bits, a glass smashed,
the thin harsh grass, and light just lasting.
A bird somewhere, utters its nervy code
over, out, over. I notice the cold.
One gun, mile off. A dulled report, and echo slighter.
Across the flash shape of the pit;
the black wheel sleeps, skyhead's stiff.
No lights over there, and all I look at
the dark is bruising; in sky and water
only a cold remainder.
The silence of dead machines,
beasts night extinguishes.

Day drives his car away. Bird's shot
or maybe sleeps; rattles fear's box again.
Only the night shifts won't soon turn to sleep,
or love in bed or lie wanting to sleep or love.
I turn to the bridge, go home.
And the little man with his little gun.
A long way off, the sun drops. And the worn things
out of sight. I mind them, strangely, like sea-stones.
Shapes hold past purpose. I can't work them out,
they ease my hand.

Not published previously, written in the 1960s

Thursday 27th October 1966: Funeral

Today we Mayor and Corporation
of Britain fly our flags half-down
the mast, but do not tear them up.

Those children are gone in the mountain-side
of slag, are dead for some black folly.
They do not shout or laugh for any piper,
'Unable to move a step, or cry.'

Make no legends for Aberfan
after what happened there
on the twenty-first of October
nineteen hundred and sixty six.

Fix no memory to name a street,
'never hear of that country more.'
Curse time, its views and monuments
for music stopped, he said, the music stopped.

"Weddings still happen here.
It's dreadful", said a woman.
"But life goes on."

Limping as before. Tomorrow live,
lift your flags high
as the smudged rope allows.

Published in *Women and Children First*,
Perkin Poets 1, 1967

Daughter In Pushchair: Early June Walk

We left the road at the humped bridge:
I carefully descend eight narrow steps,
folded pushchair in one hand,
in the other arm fourteen-month child:
one more stone ledge holds to my foot
and we stand safe on bank, to shake along
once more with unsprung rattling wheels.

Beside our motion the canal is vacant, clear
water full and silting; and the bank is empty
but for uneven stones and weed, puddles
that hold before the pushchair, as I stop.
I bend to her and we both point
to the attracting element beside us.

"Look, water": and no more than look
wanting no drowned daughter,
happy then treacherously at sea.
Though this might be a match
between clear light and light,
I would not make it, and ensure
she's safely strapped in, and I push
the noisy chair, smashing each puddle we could pass,
admiring bird and blossom everywhere.

Published in *Women and Children First*,
Perkin Poets 1, 1967

FROM *NOVEMBER PHOTOGRAPHS* 1981

Cold Night in Lancaster

Walking to town I passed the boys
who marched uphill, between the factory
their dads most likely work in
and the Catholic cathedral, towards their homes,
the stone rows they'll stay out of
till too late or bored or cold.
More purpose on their faces than mine now feels inside:
bunched as a curl-lip posse, with no enemy
that shows itself; maybe they'll join the army,
but one's too fat, two rather small and shrunk…
Woodies or time to grow? They look so old
on purpose and despite. From the great sheds
the machines' whir, the night-shift's on.
And the dull bells blur banging at practice.
Hardly seeing each other, we walk on,
so why make something of them? Why say more
than I assume already? That's their classrooms,
terraces, and likely places of employment,
and if they go to church at all, it'll be Roman.

Perhaps a touch of ghost, a memory
that serves me right, whose cause I've lost
accepting it, like everything, as common,
perhaps there's that about them…anyway
just now their uniform's their own,
they stand for nothing much.

The night's dreams are to stop the wind:
a drag, under-age pint, a bird in the bush,
nothing too posh or pearly at a guess.

So they'll keep walking, sensing the mess they're in,
exhaust the possibilities, they do it every night.
They won't win: no-one does of course,
unless those windy bells are right.
They'll grow up, marry, break the gang, drink
    legally,
work in the factory, fight maybe for their country,
    and perhaps
join the community of half-believers,
then die in revolution, crash or age. Defeat's
always predictable, it is too easy
to be right, enjoy despair.

Their losing won't put them into a rage
or Heaven, I suppose, or boards of companies.
They'll learn to live with their infirmities
of birth and breeding, work and place,
mostly shrug off their adolescent phase,
sweat for a sort of living wage,
say they believe in what they cannot understand,
support whatever kind of upper hand,
and tell their kids to never mind.

Speak

Speaklow
no-one heard.
Speakloud
won the crowd.

Speaktrue
was put away.
Speaklie
caught the eye.

Speakplain
talked to a stone.
Speaksmart
made his name.

Speakhard
was ignored.
Speakeasy
became the bard.

Sick Visitor

i.m. Frank Fairclough

Next time I go he'll be worse.
The way it is, good days get less
among the bad; most of the time
he's in bed, or propped on the couch,
and he can't want to eat. Over that
and over other things he worries,
the cut salary, the kids' play noise.
Then there are short sleeps and the hours
pain jigs in his flesh and nerves
shouting how near it's come
to rigour of death, the end of curses.
He's going out of reach of us.
He knows, envies, cares bitterly
when out of pain's worst grip and the drug haze.
Next time I go, if he's himself enough,
he'll ask me what I believe in.
I can't claim heaven's certain.
I'll say love, in some sort of way,
not punishment. There's no point in pretending
to a man in earth, living through both.
He's punished, though he's done no wrong
I couldn't match or overreach. For nothing
he's tormented, poisoned, cursed
as long as he can suffer. Cancer would do as much
if he were the worst man or the best,
letting me free for years. And he has love.
His wife will nurse him till he dies,
taking the agony and grumbling for weeks
on three or four hours sleep a night.

Her weary eyes open for him, her ears
are his, she wears his suffering always
in a plain gold band on working finger.
She will manage until this labour's done.
When his life's gone, she will feel tired and old,
at a loss, till days come round,
three children making their demands.

In The West Riding

Black stones of the dead
in thin soot-grass,
cramped slope
under the hymnless chapel.
There is no fervency now,
nothing burning on the bought land,
God's-yard, or in the dark house
pieced on the looms.

"Cross Hall Carpets" on the gate:
a stranger's shallow irony, just
a local name turned to a trade.
And a faith turned out of doors,
cutting its losses. They lie
in strange contortions of the clay.

Their richer children feed their lawns
more than they give the poor. New temples
of the living God behind each glossy door
are carpeted from wall to wall, the choir
is stereo, their faded photographs and ways
we find amusing, curious, they thought
they'd be bright angels, whom we're sure
are bones, who are our ghosts, the chill draught
that betrays the bargain underlay.

Demolition Job

In this black steepled chapel I was taught
to sing my alleluias to the king
of sky and earth and sea, all creatures' lord.
Here the demolition men are working.

A high text bade me: 'Enter His Gates With
Thanksgiving And Into His Courts With Praise.'
The painted letters set over pulpit,
loud organ, will fall to a crazed puzzle.

Grandad in his pew, home as a gargoyle
grinning high at the preacher's side. You heard
his shoe tap loud at a too long sermon.
A joke in earnest, not to be ignored.

To me then it had been there for ever,
iron and stone, white-haired ancients of days.
It might have packed souls in to the Last Trump
but has lasted less than a hundred years.

Soon the lot will have gone. Steeple, pitch-pine,
all old soldiers, every decoration
fallen from solid air, the time and space
they took room in, practising perfection.

And my old ghost, my ageing face pinches
his lines. So he at last could not kid death
though he tried. Hard by him, his blue-eyed boy,
I stood an hour, heard him work for each breath.

To build a new temple, garden parties
are busy, grand bazaars. An ideal house
displays a brass pew-number on the gate.
Nothing will grow as big and black as this.

Nor will the old man weep on high, tear hair
at my god-forsaking, most grievous fault.
Bald, easily bored with the long-winded,
takes me and angels with a pinch of salt.

One witness less in this flat crowded land
to the thrones invisible. In King Street
I cross for a last word, find 'No Entry –
Danger – Demolition' on the locked gate.

Evening in the Park

Lancaster

An evening in the park, near closing-time,
dusk gathering in the trees, high trail of vapour
dull pink, a spreading whorl.
We'd chatted with the park patrolman,
the two kids swinging, me pushing them,
one, then one. Now it was time for home,
taking a thin midge-swirl. The patrolman,
clearing the place, asks me to do a favour.
"Well, if I can." "You see this chap behind,
if you could make sure he goes on out
at the bottom gate. If not, he's sometimes there all
    night
sat in the Ladies', in case there's girls about.
A patient up the road." I agreed.
We walked on slow by the low, choked lake,
no ducks or geese to see. They yelped
at night's unease away round a corner.
So the old man came abreast, and passed,
to my muttered "Goodnight" a glint, a move in
    the eyes.
He went on by us, and I was watching him,
measuring how far to the Ladies', wondering
if he'd go in. Even the challenge had begun
to marshal in my mind: "I think you'd better
go on out, don't you? It's closing-time."

Now my eye was on him, a keeper's eye,
my talk with the kids broken, not minding them...
"Isn't the sky nothing? Isn't the world nothing?"

"The sky is, yes, but what? No, not the world. The
     world's
all kind of things. What do you think the world is?"
"Flowers, trees, blackberries…" but he had passed
     the Ladies'
and only now I saw him, a sloping walk, one leg
that flopped its foot like a deliberate clown,
reddened and restless hands that knot and loose
the fingers, straight at his sides or palm against palm
tight on his belly. He's through the iron gate,
turns right for the hospital, and we go left.
I will not turn my head to check on him.
"Yes, love, the world is all that kind of thing,
and the sky's empty, a great empty space.
Now look, we can see the moon." It is full, risen
     from the trees.
"Daddy, it's like a big round face that's watching us,
and when we move, it comes along with us."

Ironopolis

The old town's iron
stamped in a grid of streets
the dirt's drained into.
A hundred years of it.

Marks Blake noted
print out in fresh faces.
Weakness and woe
yielding their increase.

Dustbins in alleys
are slumped old men
hitting the empty bottle
on setts hard as the pension.

A blackened church, a cliff
traffic bites at, sea
persistent as profit
to build, to destroy,

must come down too
with its brick terraces;
the god has left to stay
in the securer palaces

of commerce that sprout
their bloodless towers
on each scraped site
willowherb briefly covers.

A docks wind hoops the litter
bright, irrelevant
as Indian children, laughter
a mother gives her infant.

The wind's all for change,
let's blow to a green land.
The new estate's a bandage
the sores soon stain.

Above it all airliner
lowering to ground
busy men from London
who have matters in hand.

And even higher the cold
trail of an unseen fighter
we pay to assure this two year old
his place in the gutter.

Town Centre Park: Lunch Hour

Hot day, deep into June
and all the girls, like flowers
burst bud, hold to the sun
bodies and colours. My eyes
are bees out honeying.

Idle hour turns, it turns
to hives of industry
reluctant-busy swarms.

Day's left to burn alone

and grandma bones,
put out on the step
to watch what time remains,
defrocks her knees
winks at old red hot poker of the sky
who rides cock-horse across the dirty town.

Middlesbrough, Autumn

In Laurel Street
Maple Street
in Palm and Teak
Holly and Myrtle
in planted rows off Woodlands Road
not a leaf falls.
One summer more lies dark on them.

At five o'clock, first hint of winter nights,
Fern Street's a drift of cars, deciduous
dead leaves and kids' football
scribble the spaces, blot white lines
reserved for Education Office vehicles.
It's a park, alright. The injured trees
are picked off, easy as pension parkies,
who limp, gesticulate
now the patrol car's gone.

Making a Garden

I spade into fat, wet clay
making a garden
where an old field was.
Its name divided into lots.

My excavation reveals
two years' history:
bricks, waste plastic, nails
under a dead skin of cement

slopped happy from lump trowels.
Under this, unbreathed
soil in its soured clods
the spade breaks, letting the stink out.

But I meet some worms down there:
learn how to work clay.
Go in headfirst, then
slowly digest experience.

Other men have worked this land,
witness pipe-stems, the
shards of pot, iron
tools fattened with their greedy rust.

Centuries of use, breeding.
This flower farmer
now sweats winter out
to dress up perhaps one summer.

Soon the quick December dusk
says: 'Look, a vision!'
I turn. The new house
stands out, a misplaced trick of light.

It's warm, bright, a welcoming
at the world's back end.
The night disowns it,
but it will hold the ground, settle

the cleared-off land. The thin lines
sustain it, supply
with food, warmth, clothing
to keep a hostile earth at bay.

Now dark at once, my time to
enter the mirror,
join teatime children
behind curtains, double-glazing.

When they're dug deep in dreaming,
I plot squared papers,
root in images,
make no-one's land our growing place.

Early June, Westmorland

Cool now, such common greens –
steal back the image from advertisement –
   the evening
itself, offering this lost lane,
amongst desirable villages, not for sale.

Hedge and trackside, grown one by many ways
like a people's song, a come-all-ye,
room for all in part to prosper,
species that find enough this soil, air, water.

No ordering or permits, no rights.
If we can live together, so attuned
to being, deep in all kinds of men,
our flowering selves, it is exemplary.

I see it's beautiful, this abandon
a law to self. And humans living here,
I see you're moneyed, white, you'll vote
to keep things as they're here.
The ancient park stays as a private land,
new bungalows hem in the well-kept wild.
Odd weeds in lawns prove the regime.

We'd all be country folk, pride of England,
hill-pattern lanes, the mazy hedgerows.
Who'd live in towns, where the poor's
tight rows, both pale and dark,
show how the land's now farmed?

Old Woman, Skinningrove

This was her wedding window.
Now the laced glass is gone
with salt wind, dirt in smoke,
turns round the sun.

Here she minded and mended
in one ironworks street
by a cold stained sea. A moth
in the folded blanket.

Don't take my picture, lad,
I'm too far gone for that.
She sees the end of it all,
knowing what was, is not.

Her man and babies gone,
the days that drove her tough
leave stones for air to finger,
fray the fineries off.

By Hard Hill Top

This upland moor is like any other,
empty, quiet, with sparse horned sheep,
bog-cotton, marsh-grasses, fern, heather.
That a man died on the stone road
on this side of hill, that worn soldiers,
Legion or model army, plodded here for their calling,
that quarry-carts, stone heavy, stuck in the mud,
that summer saw two lovers falling to it,
dreams of the dumb moor, would hardly matter,
matter at all. All's done and over,
leaving sheep, marsh, heather.
What I want of wilderness I make, but guess
a fly on human flesh knows only lust or tenderness
or understanding, that's of flies.
And I tramp inches over giant earth,
study the sense of scar valley, curve
of the embraced hills, locked spurs:
lost with my map of words, I call it
body, this, too large, waste, desolate,
to talk of breasts, lips, belly, raised thighs,
signs to your absent body. Between bended fells
lie spring-place and cleft course of the river.
No way to tell what drops from there, in water, blood,
rainburst and red clays. Why name the future,
child of earth and a chance seed?
What's born passes through urgency to death
while nothing's said by Hard Hill Top.
The quiet now, our busy-minding things
as seasons turn, shall we call 'Peace'?
It is a true and empty land, sleep after love.

A Late Spring, Oakley Walls

The unmoved ash, a wrestler
rooted to this moor. It has never
pinned the adverse air
to a fall. So far
it has kept its feet.

The white gales grappled it,
a right match, not yet done.
They have melted,
are resting this season.
Now to their fine-sky shadow-fighting
the low flying jets return.

It will take all comers
in the many bended boughs,
sways tentacles in air's deep swell.
Bark-braided, thick-set trunk, a bruiser.
From knuckles of bud
it will spring light-fingers
in its own good time.

From sky's high surfaces
those quickfire-silvers
are best not diving down
to this ground-stander.
The smartest fighter,
proud cock of air and fire,
could drown in the green clutching.

The ash waits. If it will come,
it will come. There is
no expecting victory,
no longing for summer.

Words Cannot Express

for my father

How pat this train's at the door
when you are dead, it is
decked out with pale flowers,
saynowt verses for the hour of need.

How full the carriages are:
so many of your pals, they've
found themselves nearer
now you're for the grave.

What should they have to say?
It is enough they come
seeing they too will die,
face these black-coated men.

And you stare, under the set lid-stones,
dumb as you'd sit for hours
bored and stiff with pain
in the fag-end of your years.

Mum's cleared the cabinet
of the labelled bottles of pills,
the balms named after saints:
the dustbin is full of spells

well-meant for the mended arm,
the sawn end of leg,
the ulcers that bled in your belly.
You even gave up your cigs.

Your hopes lodged in your sons
who, resenting that,
would snap, look weary, groan
at your need to know how we did.

The chances you had missed
you'd order for us to take,
glow for any success,
report it to mates in the park.

Dad, I couldn't have told you
the half of it, you'd have died!
And there's no point now,
a coffin confession's not needed.

Perhaps you see all that is done:
if the minister's right, you'll be there
in a heaven I can't imagine
having a right good stare,

sat smoking at the front window
watching for what will pass.
Leave off, live your own happy-ever-after,
don't waste any eternity on us.

But if, just dead, you're set to turn to clay,
change for the underground,
nothing that I can say
will make you comprehend

how, heir to this face in the mirror,
I see you off, a father his son.
Mind how you go round Dangerous Corner,
best not come back once you've gone.

Stone Crosses, Goathland Church

The church-field, in a bowl of the high moor,
is thronged with starlings, they thicken the ties
to weathercock's stub mast. Memorial stones,
green with a crust of lichens, slowly tilt
to the land's long tide, which carries the dead
and will cover the named stones, drink them down.

These monuments with their inscribed words
    demonstrate
that we do not forget, are remembered,
a huddle of small craft in safe harbour.
Even an anchor hooks into marble,
'Thy Will Be Done' set clear cut down the spine,
above one married pair's last double bed.

Now where's the use in that? No storm of life
will blow them from their daily course, who are
William, Elizabeth, fifty years dead.
Was it a hymn, perhaps their favourite,
that left, land-locked for centuries, on them
this anchor? Is it "grounded in the Love"

these crosses crowd in to persuade that I
should accept again? The saving sacrifice,
an inhuman pattern of a man, 'Thy Will'
that public passion, which should make love stick.
I would argue with this, wrestle to a fall,
Jacob at Peniel, blessed with disbelief.

But the bad dream touches my nerve, I see
your much-loved mortal body out of breath,
crippling under stone, without a hope of
any life to come. Enough to shake me.
From drowned soul-sailors, safe in clay's slow curve,
I hurry back to living company.

That night we drank late in the hotel bar,
gregarious, convivial, unsure,
if we had thought about it, where we sailed,
drops in the ocean, night as deep as stars.
Then look-out, mindful of you home in bed,
I counted graves, till sleep took me for dead.

November Photographs

The days get shorter, sunlight's echoes dying,
the journeys out of, into night
repeated on the urban routes.
But solstice turn will come, sun grow again,
promote Greek Islands, the South of France,
bronzed and indolent images.

November's a ship to desert, no bare breasts
to be poached on its dim, chill decks,
a set for melancholic fashion,
a ghost of months, and with a ghost's persistent
visiting: I am rarely rid
of its reminders, even en route
to Le Soleil. In every case the last laugh
is the rotter's, who imposes
his heads on all my framed coinage
intended for purchase of stopped sun, held time:
wedding album, the blue yonder,
all our astonished poses.

One day I would settle this melancholy
turning the light's trick against it,
get perspective and true colours.
A filmed record that should exorcise the ghost
from three unseasonal quarters.
One day gave me four photographs.

All through the night a sharp frost bit at the ash
and all night leaves, the last left, fell
down the still air. So I found them

driving in as the sun gave a first hard stare:
that great green surge broken, a dry
spring in the round, stale pool of tears.

In the mirror, lunch-time, all their shopping done,
young mothers guide laden pram-teams
uphill from town. At half a mile
their anoraks are bright as brief bikinis
in a shade of the last summer
in the fenced close garden-patches.

Curtains for a brilliant sky. The radio
throbs at the high pitch, distorting
car's choaoaural evensong;
I just catch, set in the pudding-basined hedge,
the one bare tree's black skull, black bones
on screen, the last footage of light.

Night's drawn in, I find the car iced with glitter,
the same road repeats the same tree
for the headlamps to fasten on:
it is a white root groping up sunless sky
so buds may burst unnatural,
fire-light in a deep seam of coal.

I could puzzle polite company with these;
you see, November's figuring
my mind's springs, corruptly rooted
in dead dark. Let there be available light!
The kids will clear the old haunt with
one bonfire, winter in the sun.

Ward Three

They have lived here so long,
in the hospital of this earth,
in the corridors of this century.
Grown old, they are weary, powerful
over everything they no longer handle.
Born at just that turn, and there were
so many others in just those places,
the survivors of so many centuries.

Their breeding was on Ward One.
Their textbooks were old men's errors.
Their drink was the blood of other young fools,
their bread was the many hungry in their peoples
and their game war: they turned
the glass globe over,
making the snow shudder.

Their lessons were learned,
they put childishness away.
Desire ruled with circumspection,
a blameless life; with training
they got hands dirty and clean
and all else required of them.

Ward Two they found prepared for them,
it would set them up for life.
They had the freedom of the place,
builders of ruins, builders of firestorms,
architects of peace. A blind eye
to botched and monstrous surgeries,

no wrong on their gloved hands.
These are the days they remember.

Then how did they come
to Ward Three, to be penned
deep in these safe shelters?
They play bright lights on the video screen,
buttons at their stiffening fingers.
They trust no nurses nor the drugged facts fed them.
It is what they are left with
to see out their time.

Blood taking leave of the brain
with the first giant reflexes,
the habit of appetites.
What should we expect of children
asked, at the finish,
to begin all over again?

Uncollected Poem

Jumping the Queue

Your best foot forward.
In whose shoes you'd like,
but get in the queue,
this is where it all starts,
civilisation begins right here.

The first were for school dinners:
the sirens sounded off all through last lesson,
then you queued, smelling food faint and cold
at the far end. You'd never make it,
your emptiness would cave in,
wrinkle, a burst balloon-skin.
The hatch comes into sight at last,
but then a clutch of teachers pushes in
and you were in the queue again
while they had more of everything.
One time we moaned. Our tutor said
it was all part of growing up,
if you didn't queue, you might get in
before the ones always in front.

We queued for life, growing up where we stood:
in silent strings for school assemblies,
for buses that came late, for films in cold, grey rain.
We studied, Fox and History,
our Twentieth Century, its millions in queues
for a cup of meal, for the last train out,
for the bath-houses. The dead stand in their lines

staring in silence at our careless eyes.
They fill high shelves in library basements.

After school, we changed tense for the future
and found that queues were back in fashion
though not much in the news, no cameras here,
not even much to talk about
until some joker asked the right silly question:
"What are we all doing in this queue?"
We soon forgot the question in the answers
learning for example
what we all had in common, like
no money, hungers, sick pets
(that was in the PDSA queue),
fears in the night and a united
bloody great fed-up-ness
with queueing all your life.
For what? To die at the front.
She told me how to mend my broken bike.
I swapped with how to back a winner...
now and again.

Then we came onto queues, who designed them,
how them that designed them always seemed to...
sorry, in a hurry!
How to stop them, how to
teach ourselves some tricks,
how to change the rules.

So now you're thinking to yourself:
"What, just by standing in a queue and talking,
weight on your feet, time on your hands?"
It was that simple,

but people can be prejudiced against great truths,
even the highly-thought-of can fail there.

The other night I went to my kid's school
to hear the head, who moped on for too long
to those who'd gone to listen
about parental interest and its lack,
and then to stand in queues
to listen to the verdicts from them that know.
I started on the parents, queue by queue,
told them to try it, having their say,
working it out together, two or three families
with a couple of teachers, see if that worked better,
changed things for the good. That kept them busy,
so I went for the head and pointed out
the error of his thinking to that day,
explained this linear stuff in education
deadening as the dole,
how he should let the children
talk, mostly that, using the teachers when needed,
in their proper place, a civil service.
I thought I'd got him through, to see that maths
was easier when you talked, that little groups
plotting their revolutions
(scientific, literary, political)'s the stuff
of learning and that lines of desks can never…
really thought I'd said enough, pressed into him
the print of a new age.

I learned next day how little I'd achieved,
how I couldn't match
the strength of training, ink thick on his brain.

Next day our kid came home with *Parents' News*.
The headline promised us: PLEASE NOTE NEW
   RULES.

No Talking Nine To Four.
No Groups Of Two Or More.
No Parents Through This Door.

He hadn't understood a word I said
and missed the chance
to have the best school in the town,
gushing with self-made people,
full of a common sense of a new world,
fit to start making it.
But I won't forget:
those kids who're in his ruler's reach
will soon be stuck in queues,
ready to jump. I'll wait.

Published in Crossing the T's, ed by Bob Pegg, Cleveland
Arts, 1985

FROM *A COLD SPELL* 1996

Potato Sellers - Cleveland

Through wasted lands, the major routes
display, in lay-by, on grass-verge
the advance guards, these far-flung ends
of profit, enterprise, advantage.

Fifty miles north the Wall's abandoned,
poems and sheep and not a toss for Rome;
twenty miles south the squat of Fylingdales
warning the riggs and cairns of what's to come.

And here these foot-men have to live, and now
without a hope of proper work or pride,
a laid-on, paid-off casual regiment
that's bought and sold and taken for a ride.

Such forlorn openings, some general's joke
among the derelicts of heavy losses.
A bag's price standard, shelter plastic sheet,
killed hours to breathe in luck's exhausted gases.

Cold furnaces stand cracked, the speechless din
of radio-babble towers another day
till watch ends, lights out, nothing to report.
A kestrel beats time to its dangled prey.

Old Workings
Howe Bridge

It's the leisure centre, Sunday morning
as the tangled knitting of so many swimmers
drops into one bright bowl of flesh and drink.

Including this early shift of retired pitmen,
blue traced beneath pale rind. They laugh in a round
to be grown wrinkled, to rise above ground, under
    water.

Hair like damp towels, licking crisps and chlorine
from awkward cavities, on water-legs we walk the
    car-park.
Three islands break the crust of this dead sea's
    horizon.

The first heaped pitdirt, unregenerate, squat on its
    hunkers;
then one still blackened but a penitent, bowed on
    the bench.
This last new-born, a tame hump, a greenswardy
    sepulchre.

Marked for life, did you say? Lord, I don't think so.
Colliers and collieries the dust bites for good, given
    time.
Folk only remember when a house sinks, a road
    slides under.

Oakley Walls

I

The farm's old grassyard in its idle years
sweet with flowers, sits all day with me
wedged in the side of hill
above the working acreage,
under the bracken moor.

Shining, hurled bark of earth,
that bole thick-ringed with years.
Under this summer's day, beneath mind's sod,
its deepest probing roots, first warm seas sway,
lost rivers maze through swamps, rock-beds
are shuffled like dominoes, pile, tip, crack,
and molten tholeite squeezes out
a burning ditch from Mull to Ravenscar.
For a god's hands a day's work:
Who casts the dice, obeys the cast
to test a crazy system, prove a futile skill
in folding strata, planing them with seas,
folding again; with hermit-juggler's sleight
lifting the landmass, conjures out fresh streams
to scratch initial sketches for this dale
that opens to me its mapped detailed surfaces.

Thought digs with the mole
under the skin of grasses,
squats time-stunned, earth-blinded
as millions of years in a dark second pass
to the last ice-age. Then this wide dale's

a lake of melted snows the thick ice fists have
    dammed
pressing up Esk to Lealholm, from the low Vale of York
up Leven to Kildale, but got no passage here.
Rich silts, a slow black rain,
sifted the flood, settled to the valley.
The line of hill-farm houses, moor walls,
marks the shore.

Next into the game throw men
come here to hunt and farm,
reasoning the advantage.
Here begin history and language,
as common poets give natural accidents
a meaning and a name.

Pebbles of all their livings litter the soil
time has poured on them, fracturing pot,
fattening iron with rust.
Engineers' works are rotted, lost in later walls,
tarred over, though a few stay sainted
relics for week-end pilgrims – will a touch
cure the present? – who just hear
last echoes of the mingling languages.
The TV mast winks in the dark on Bilsdale
and Wilton's waste-gas torches tint the sky.
The Ordnance Survey, studied in the schools,
a sad, fixed poem, plot of the dead's imaginings.
On Fylingdales, far as I see from here,
lowering like alien spacecraft
three shining domes
and Phantom jets that shave the few bent trees
then twist, climb, loop in mated patterns,

dismember birdflight, warn me of this:
what's coming is a game like all that's gone.
Two reasoning men can now bring down earth's tree
in half an hour into a last jigsaw,
leaving no chance to piece it up,
all seeds crumbled inside themselves.
Even the fern fails
after that fire on the moor.

II

A cold, damp autumn night, past thought of holidays.
I should sleep for work, I fool with prophecies.
Tomorrow I shall practise faith in betterment,
the education of our young, the future's front-line
    hopes,
set out more duck-boards they can walk along,
who from so early play with guns and bombs,
learn murder's swings and ropes. So I go on
starting to spin all fates,
but hear one baby calling in her dream,
wild bird we chance in the storm,
and think, out over night, to the farm,
how our children sparked its tinder,
their flashing eyes, loud din
giving its body pulse and breath again,
raised up dead branches into garden trees
and grew a house in the field-head
from the seeds of fallen stones.

When another evening's gone
and all of us with it and all ours,
and an old isolate, time on his hands,

clears off the board and sets another game,
when Wilton is dark and content as the tumuli
and that sweet, sturdy house is under ash or ice,
it will not matter.
Poverty Hill needs no name.

To the dark Beacon a blind wind tells the year's death,
no live wild thing complains.
This family sleeps; by Emily, half-read, *The Long Winter*.
Warm in suburban house, draped in an old white scarf,
she bent with storied age and told the cosy cat,
'Lots of snow, Sherbet, lots of snow.'

You Can't Beat 'Em

On a wet Wigan wall
down which seven slates have slipped
leaving this rain a hole
four TETLEY BITTERMEN
are propped with pints and confidence.
They are not sorry for themselves at all.

A Haunting

for Hilda and Rob

The house is empty of them,
I am to clear the rest of it
and cut out a first clearing,
make camp in their belonging.

The night wind brushes, brushes
at the trees' dark, brittle hair,
echoes as only my foot falls
through the closing chill.

The living room's my bolt-hole:
its gas-fire sparks and flames,
cracks out these perished bones,
warms ghost, its night-flit done.

There is enough haunting here.
Our younger bodies touch, are frit
to speak, are frit to love for care
we'd skittle out the fast asleep upstairs.

Tonight they are past all waking,
I lay face down their photographs
that look on through me, blankly refuse
to let these tired eyes close.

Voices I hear are not more
than the push of air carries
through the window's skim of glass.
The telephone is out of use.

At first light I will put on flesh,
hump boxes on to other destinies,
decamp with my lost soul, leave
the house to fill with its next life.

A68 North

Look, given time, every despair turns quaint,
trees age to fancy's images, hard words
translate to catch-eye road-sign curios.

Glory of scrubbed light shines, now there's no pain.
Consett is a changed vision, no hell-fire
to scare off pastorals, the world's made new,
the ash-heaps rounded off to a likeness.
Next the grafts, the green skins of surgery.

By picnic places, rustic bench and board,
by the waters of Tyne, pass on, no place
for weeping, let old familiar tales
lull you soft, consider the brochures
of all abandoned livings. In the earth
such revolutions, these few poor traces.

Only the words grip to their speakers' soil,
have let go meaning but not let go hold.
They bend to the governing wind, mimic
the hills' changes, black, red, grey, green.
From a last battle, old grave, new settlement
the places' birth-names twisted to these part-clues,
the broken curses, voided promises.

Only the words, rubbed raw as deal by rain,
survive as spells we mutter as we pass.

In Conference

I am looking out, the window
to a wider understanding
beyond all this paper talk
on the fifth floor of *The Imperial*
and there is clear evidence that
these Harrogate chimney pots
are in charge, manage the great sky
and its unknowing hosts,
their swell and their migration.

Though it is done without a flicker,
laid down with the stones,
without questioning of destiny,
a century of smokefall
dark on the parapets up here
for us all to admire,
at the top, in the *Empire Suite*,
the unchanging arrogance
of crowns on high-set heads.

If the sun screams of fire or the clouds
shake in revolutionary dance,
these chimney pots are in charge, they manage
the great sky, at whose eye-rim
a green tide lifts. Hills, woods and dales.

There we learn to swim, begin in that flesh
to speak the language of the deep,
welcome its overwhelm, the toppling at last
of chimney pots, this Harrogate regime.

Visitors

Do we still live in there,
this house with a chill
in it, which our devout will
managed in duty, with care?

Pictures, music and books
wait in the wall's long line
for visitors who might sign
in our hands' known strokes.

The winter's drizzle of dust
is grimly settling in,
the siege might be lifted with spring,
swept aside with one gust.

But the house is a house
of the dead, we have to live
where we can make believe
to accommodate our loss

of the fabric's word,
what was inherited,
ingrained, so we had thought,
loss of a settled creed.

Not crowned with promised crowns,
in our joined bodies' tent,
unfurnished, easily rent,
here we have laid our bones.

Admiring the bright stars pour
down the sky's slow race,
we have found ourselves a space
dispossessed, nowhere.

And this house with its cold stone
must be entered and left with care
for those still asleep in there
who may wake some time, find us gone.

Successors

Half-term, a day trapped in the Offices:
the schools are emptied, the children poured
into shopping centres, arcades, parks and terraces.

Thirty years' work, youth's learning still the dream
of the waking business that draws out my hours.
Today it's battle with a distant acronym

by fax and phone - fire, sword are out of stock,
filling a questionnaire for some obscure research
and, as school's out, taking a lunch-time walk

to the post office. In the ragged zigzag queue
the wiser mothers clutch their offspring's hands,
in spite of wailed entreaty won't let go.

They've sadly learned, out through the swing-
    door's grab
are plain clothes monsters, other mothers' kids,
who live for their ambition, it's the job

of the scissorman, snip snap they'll do for
any unlucky one, always expecting to pull
unstuck some safely delivered toddler.

Such horror's not our business. Banner wavers
for excellence, achievement, golden futures,
we urge them forward with crisp wads of favours,

in step, next generation, our successors.
Leaders and teachers have to give creed out loud
as witnesses for progress, which pays us.

They are determined, destined to succeed
where we have sunk, to be the earth's last hopes,
march full of promise, arrive, keep the word.

But it is half-term, there is time for doubt,
for pessimistic brooding when the phones don't ring,
for wondering what this life is all about.

Sat at my desk I fear these paper flowers,
as foolish, scared and brave in their front line
as all that went before, will fall in mothers' tears.

And they, quite right, don't give a damn for me,
get on with learning what they need to know,
how to escape their guards, take life, risk poetry.

Elegy, St. Patrick's Day 1992, Thornaby
for Noel Lally

Work's ended and I'm driving home
into the west and setting sun
that blinks its blinders at me on the road
through these dark slats of cloud.

They stretch out in their long pew rows
with grey heads bowed and full of tears
as us today, packed in the requiem church
with your deserted body in its box.

Let my eye leave the daily route, rise
over estates of factories and houses,
hurl over school, church, river of Thornaby
and seek you in the distances of sky,

climb up the dales of Tees and Swale,
skim the old Celtic fortress hills,
fall with the Lune and out across Bay sands,
and in your native Ireland come to ground.

Noel, you'd shake your head at so much fuss
made over you, make mock of stuff so curious
as poems about you, flights of a driver's eye
taken off the road. So, instead, a summary.

You were as sure of heaven as anyone, backed it
with all you had, lived for your favourite.
And made us see the joke in, learn to laugh
at what Creation tripped us with. Is that enough?

Going down now, of all day the most bright
since it began, the smile of the light
making these many weeping faces radiant.
"Jaysus" you might have said. And meant.

Redcar Saturnalia

They go berserk, the little devils,
midwinter's dark perform their revels.

So on the shopping precinct wall
at one foot wide and six feet tall

a penis stands erect in paint,
was daubed on last night, is a quaint

reminder from a pagan age
to put all Redcar in a rage.

See how brightly shine its balls
and how this tinsel tree appals

every adult's only eye,
recognising their young fry

ready to betray that folly,
their begetting. They put holly

round the stem, green spray leaf
and red spray berry, showed the grief

of mistletoe, demonstrated
passion's prick, that the much hated

sexual love comes to its flower in pain,
then falls away to rise again,

is the first tree in the green wood,
the born again, the resurrecting god.

There's not a shop in Redcar that would stock it:
children tell teacher of the smashing rocket!

From the Holiday Village
for Jutta and Manfred, Gartow, Summer 1989

Elbuferstrasse signs me to the tourist route
along the river-bank: here the Elbe divides
one people to two states so far through five decades.

Under the rim of dykes the marshland is reclaimed
for farms, for small wild things, also for us
who are mostly German, mostly visitors.

Protected, we may swim or fly, hunt, watch, escape,
all bookmarked species busy on the *Wanderweg*.
I goggle at a crane's take-off, almost belly-flop,

then, settled beneath spruce and old oak
to catch the woodpecker drumming its bit of ground,
guess at the shadow language of the Wendland.

Twin television masts on the slight rise of Hohbeck
spill images' excess across defensive wire:
only the approved monochrome makes it back over.

No crowds are found here at newstime border posts.
The bridges blown in '45, *"Bahn stillgelegt"*,
and Highway 191 near Kaltenhof can't reach

across to their dry land. Bombs broke its back
to put a stop to that. We have to leave the car
and walk the spans that cross the flood-plain, stare

at the two stranded piers, nearer marked *"NAZIS
    RAUS"*,
the fence on that side, another concrete watch-tower,
the town behind the trees that was familiar.

"Ich hatte einst ein grosses Vaterland"
penned on the bars at the end of this road
sounds more lament than motto for a sword

kept safe for Siegfried. Gods secretly decreed
the river here, slicing up war's spoil,
the agony of broken words, split, spilt, *zerstreut*.

What can time heal, no wounds like these to show?
One place I'm told to look across Elbe, use my
    binoculars,
a German in his fifties, and my eye follows

his keen finger. "The watch-tower?" "Not the
    watch-tower!
To the left, before the clump of trees. Just look."
I see, a yard inside the wire, the nest, the young stork.

For November

At the affair's end
here is a love-letter,
a last fling of the sap
to the sun, a world away.
Burn this and remember.

We warm hands and faces,
blind with the blink of light.
We become all flame, the image
roped to the broken chair.
We have the gift of fire,
its babbling tongues.
We have to eat all winter.

After Our Kind

We have, yes, had children
and look, how they have grown
so you would hardly know them.

To see ourselves in there gets
by the year more staring,
they walk off with everything.

Happy to watch them go we'd
neglect those left back here.
Perhaps as well to take care.

****

Till we get to funerals,
wills, such stuff in the brain,
let's people the world again.

But be content with poems,
precocious images
of how it is between us

when we shrug at our years,
join in a springing rush
off the high board, make our splash.

****

Left alone to sort papers,
you might read of it, page
on dry page, as you arrange

to leave things tidy for them
who'll pick up your pieces.
Poems? They'll be in creases!

There at that last look, puzzle
to place the lost nights that
got into print this our lot.

****

Will you tell them apart then?
Wonder where they have gone
leaving only you to mourn?

Sunsets

at the end of my mum's street are a treat,
but in the doorhole night,
dragging its feet, has come all the same
to re-possess our light.

So once a sky all beams and squalls
like me in *The Firs*, a new babby,
about nowt much, not more nor less
than milky teat or mucky nappy.

And this now with its pillar of cloud
fire-red, a grate of ash-glow,
a plane dropping to Ringway through evening
with a bright flashlight belly.

The visitor to my own flat town,
a dull street where nothing much surprises,
soon no-one will speak of your story.
What have I to say to this?

The most spectacular end to any cul-de-sac I know
when there's all-clear in Wigan's sad Atlantic skies:
the vapours drying from the brick,
the dust-sheets shaken off and folded.

I can't let go this long and ordinary enduring.
You will give everything away,
even now thump upstairs
to dig for something the kids might like.

You will have the house emptied
boot-load by boot-load.
One week from here and you are restless
for this ascetic order.

Always someone else who is worse off
and signals from window to window
when the Witnesses walk the street,
when somebody spots subsidence or smells gas.

So this place is to get older, I've to leave you here
with three clocks telling different times.
If you die first, I'll not be back
unless to give a talk, present prizes.

Though now I need more years to reach inside me,
for you to tell me riddles, tidy your garden,
to mind her next-door, to keep on watch
for furies that are best locked-out.

Time to learn something to carry me through,
this eavesdropper in on your street,
strange car that is there then gone again
in the worst and best dreams.

You got no daughter who might pick the lock,
the saving grace of your love's grieving:
with this son there is still a contract
not to break the heart open.

You let the tears run away, sane as drainpipes,
admire the calendar of sunsets,
half-singing those crimson hymns,
winding and not resetting your three clocks.

Hotel with Headphones

"Ah! Talor del tuo pensiero venga un foglio messaggero e la vita fuggitava di speranze nutriro"
(Callas sings Lucia di Lammermoor, Staatsoper, Berlin, 1955)

The bar deserted for the single bed
and arias tracked to occupy the brain,
the text to weight the lids, its matter is

that my tongue seeks you out, wants to winkle
the essence from all your hiding holes.
All this pit-toil I expend in your flesh,

down the dark drift-mines, to snatch you up
in one cry, then dance you there on the tip.
Bravura, the lip of the light!

This singer lays siege to my solitary,
rain rapples at the window, is not heard.
In this mute, lonely auditorium

I am host to a dense prefiguring
of some last losing, no more spark in us.
I watch along the corpse to the far toes.

But here's your head bent to my little book,
your breast spilled ore, melt to my mould,
the flexing fell-track of your spine.

And where you watch, there your tongue seeks me out.
Across high England, its abandoned workings,
pulls the strong held cord of the song.

The Little Pot

i.m. Frances Horovitz

My hands could crack it as a nut,
the fingers tight against its ribs,
this little pot, this shell
rippled in the clay-waves.

Before the potter pulled it out,
pummelled and clawed it out, it lacked all echo,
was not a pebble, not a root, not a bone.
It has the greens of moss in damp air.

Work of her claws, she gave it
her name, painted that scissors on the base,
bathed in a bitter green wine,
baked it to brittle-hard.

Now it squats in your house,
a little pot to gather the dust,
left to lie with purpose or neglect
on a high shelf or a cluttered sill.

One winter's end, who knows when,
the sun's skin still pale,
glaze-green tendrils will claw out,
put one black kiss on the light.

A *Johnston's Readyfold*

This Coloured Touring Map,
a *Johnston's Readyfold*:
note that 'y', shows it about our age:
consider its creases, tattered ends,
its sure vein-tracery, lack of motorways.
Rescued from the title of junk
this scrap of endeavour,
why do I give it you?

I'm prompt to the argument
the gift does not require.
I recognise in you
a part-deliberate, part-casual
loser and finder of your way;
you see me as a maker
of straight roads,
arriver at destinations.
Which of us knows us, which?
I know each minds the other,
needs to learn what's harder,
to love the trackless self.

I will own this description:
a maker of coloured maps,
rather one map, our region,
much like the land laid here,
the limits not differing much.
One who won't reach to world's ends,
eschews chimeras, knows the terrain's plots,
this little patch of souls,
this middle age's ravelling of routes.

We've run to this to meet ourselves
as histories, anachronisms
escaped from our framed photographs
on parents' mantelpieces.
We stand together, in small company,
gaze on the shifts of sky,
out of our founding time.

Admiring our survival we could become
too reverent before old maps and such.
Nostalgia gives lie to the need, to get
from that we were to what we yet might be.

Our land's built up of images,
words for this tree, that fell, these fields.
Black Sike, Summer Wood, Low Moor, Long Side.
We own no ground and make no lasting claim.
Each has to find a new road every time
or lose some chance of joy, transient landscape.

I'm lost in rambles now.
Time to come down, complete
my presentation, end the essay.
To use the Readyfold,
open out and turn the leaves
to move to north or south,
refold, use like a book.
And read me like a map
that's growing out of date,
covers this lonely land, often
getting it wrong, trying to comprehend
dark fell and limestone cleft,
streams that flow underground.

At Castle Howard

I look him in the eye, that white
the caretaker re-touched last winter,
big house's "little blackamoor".

Whose is the face he is the witness for
above the hearth, under a tarry picture,
unrestored smuts of paleskin gods?

He stares from the fireplace stone,
is a toothy gargoyle in the gut
of this imposing family's shrine,

African boy. Howardian pet in silks?
Footman in some dead Venetian's
court? Who took his name?

I can remember him in this
wandering Italian art, can see
he went on grinning at the flames.

****

If the lot had burned sky-high
I'd not know now, not care
that he had gone down with

all hands, without distinction,
heaped dust in the crematorium,
day-labourers, slaves, artisans.

I can't startle up, can't spot
who made what I pay to admire,
argosies' plunder beached in history.

Their tools are worked to rust,
gone on the fire, or into the rise of earth:
trowels, barrows, thimbles, spades.

The ceremonial fakes, inscribed
in silver, never put to use,
clutter the gallery's glass cases.

****

From all that kindling
I snatch out one more story,
an unnamed Amerindian girl.

Atlantic distances divide
their shackled continents,
joined in this English grave.

Chinaborros de aguja
the work of her bone-needle,
four months from her fingers' life,

hammock of feathers stripped
from toucans, parrots, rainbow humming-birds,
to rub the spark of patron's appetite:

"... which notwithstanding
its humble origins will I hope
be found worthy a place ..."

Driving from *Lear* in Snow

Now we must, audience, all of us, enter
a night not fit for kings, those made mad,
all who are wretched, can no longer listen.
We learn here, perform here our journey
from a dark, shuttered house, through that
same universe, to an uncertain welcome.
The car warms up, the screen demists, radio
sputters out its early hours' bravado. The road

shrinks to a single file, snow thickening
the outer lane, through a hopeless world
the wind bawls over. Tail lights, head-lights linked
in our near-blind pilgrimage, weary of finding
the sign for home and willing some way out,
any crazed edge, sheer as an angel's fall,

we'll be waved on down by some pretending fiend
in a solemn dance, a blue shivering light.
There's now no reasoning my brain's ice-daze,
no word of consolation in the heart,
it spites love's promises. So head and cold
breast-stone move forward comfortless
in this most open ground, where the wind
can't be imagined, the snow never finds rest.

Slumped at my side in sleep, familiar
traveller, your name is, you are one
in the night's great grave. Nothing to offer you
at dawn's final strangeness, a waking word of grief
or anger or farewell. Hands grip the wheel,
road's clear, the storm gives up its dead.

A Cold Spell

First light, there's no mistaking
the blackbird in its garden,
the bright nail of its beak
stabbed at a horizon
of ice-scraped branches,
with the promise of harm
in its birthright clamour,
claiming sufficient ground
or else or else or else.

Such a cold spell, so early,
stretched out from northern Russia
across the fields, yards, gardens
deep with buried hopes,
marching the dialects of blackbirds
to fill these English roads at dawn
with the stiff queues of refugees.

The bitter season's greetings,
blackbird in a garden of snow,
hugged in a cast-off jersey
always too tight at the neck
like a conscience, like a uniform.
Again the innocent's part,
the preparation for birth,
the requisition of death.
I, says the blackbird.

At twilight an exchange of fire,
sortie and retreat, low swoops

over borders, the trampled lawns
that were their playgrounds.
Children called in
who will never come.

Back home, in the warm,
do not doubt the blackbird,
bred for the implacable future,
dug in under the hedge
against this next long night.

Uncollected Poem

Tractor and Plough
Eden Valley, 2000AD

Tractor and plough
turn the year
from then to now,
from there to here.
Ten hundreds come
to one bright day.
Turn the year,
tractor and plough,
all that same,
that shining clay.

FROM *WINTER BREAKS* 2006

The Baker

I learned not to believe a word he said.
It didn't always work, but they're like that,
granddads, not quite grown up yet, not quite
playing the rules, not quite to be trusted.

The one I had lived in a baker's shop,
he was the baker, sold his backyard bread
in the downstairs front-room, buttered it
with Woodbines, Mint Imperials, bottled pop.

He let this grandson wander everywhere,
scullery, kitchen, landing. I could go
in the front parlour, play with the piano,
enter the shop, steal from the toffee jar.

In the long baking shed that filled the yard
were dusty sacks to sift white fingers in,
gas griddles quiet, waiting for the sign
to lift crisp muffins from the flour and lard.

But not the cellar. Dangerous, he warned,
catching me once too often at the sneck,
creaking the door ajar, sniffing the dark,
its pungent pool that lapped the top step's land.

'Why is it dangerous, Granddad?' 'Because,
my lad, of lack of light, the steep drop down,
the dead chap underneath his chiselled stone
in the flagged floor, and still one more because:

the well, just covered with a broken door,
so deep it could go down to endless night.'
I had to see all that, Jack Shiney-Light
and Granddad guiding the black-out tour.

I don't recall much else of that descent,
perhaps a smell of timber-damp, brick-mould,
a rusty hook that scratched, thick webs that fold
over the eyes, shadows that bent and bend

fifty years on to shroud me. A body,
was there, under that lettered stone? A well?
Never got down again, so I can't tell
the truth from tales with that old Methody.

I see now, in that dark, ghosts fetched from France.
Those dusty heaps are stockpiled newly dead
or sacks of loaves his kitchen cannot feed
to no-more-hungry mouths, wanting the chance

that limped him home, the shrapnel in his spine,
alive, to wife and son, chapel and shop
below which we two started on our drop
down planking steps into that sea-coal-mine

of our imaginings, while all around
and under us real pitmen bent and cut
and propped their tunnelling through fossil dirt
and trawled the airless nightmares of the drowned.

The shop still serves, with the front parlour added,
as off-licence. Teetotal George can't turn
in narrow plot. He won't root out his son,
wife, daughter-in-law on top or mum and dad

tucked in below. 'Not a dead cert, not quite,
miladdo. Suppose the dark is just the trick
light plays, tickled like me that look-a-like
shines his flashlamp down this shut, flooded pit.'

The Strap

Leather strap on the back door nail.
He'd belt us if we were naughty,
but never. We didn't know.
Never was future, moon-landings, our own cars.
Strap - shiny till you got close, saw
the cracks and scabby bits. His chin was like that
before he shaved. Hot water from the geyser,
the brush and shaving stick. And he kept on
looking and stroking. I do that with my beard.
Good lads most the time, our mum said.
Wouldn't have let him use it anyway.
But never. I sometimes think
just once he'd have enjoyed it, realised
he could do something. Not just work,
snooker, Woodbines, the pictures.
Thought I saw him once with another woman
five rows in front, got up, went home, forgot.
Did he? Did I dream?
Did the thought of her bare arm cross his mind
when the second ulcer burst?
By then mum and dad had moved and we
had wives and kids and lived away. The strap
went in the bin.
I wish they had had more excitement.
My kids look at me.
I wonder what they'll wish they'd wished for me
when it's quite safe, doesn't matter anyway.

Martha

We knew the cracks of every paving stone
down the back yard. Familiars in slow motion,
they told us nothing new, repeated jokes
every time we linked arm up in arm
and made procession to the outside lav,
silent as picture heroes flickering
through every weather the Lord God could chuck
at your rheumatics. How He'd tweak your bones,
climatic osteopath, to Whom you'd sing
Charles Wesley's anthems gritted through false teeth.
I almost had to lift you up the steps,
so you could shuffle round the door in boots
of black, that took ten minutes' bending down
to lace, and later that was my job too.
You wore them every day that you were up
and sitting on your chair-commode, a doll
dressed in long frock, clean pinnie, with your hair
in two tight plaits, braided across your head.
Eighteen and a prop forward, I could have
picked your skinny weight straight up and galloped
over the line, touched down between the posts,
but pain had got possession in the ruck.
Our kitchen stewed all those long summer days
with you, your bed, the pot-containing chair,
the sick-sweet smell that Dettol could not hide.
Teeth grinning underwater on the sill,
for eight slow weeks you did not take a bite,
but just drank milky tea and drooled and drooled,
hour upon hour, a long, unbroken skein
into the bucket nested on your lap

beneath the lump that grew, its thick grey fluid.
Talk had got stuck, you had to grunt and point
to tell us you had done for now. Buckets
had to be emptied too, and gradually
we were flushing you away, and always
your face was as pink and plain as a child's,
the lamentation only now arrives
after forty years' journey, grips as cold
as winters over Saddleworth's black hill.
You heard the news of my state scholarship
and gave a tiny smile, nod, touch of hand,
then slept again, your white unplaited hair
on the white pillow, while we ate our tea.
I half-heard movement in the night, but slept
weary with digging, mowing, marking-out
in parks and cemeteries and playing fields.
Dad woke us early, told us you had died
peaceful. Already you were gone, they'd thought
it best. But when you were brought back, they let
us look a minute into the coffin
where you lay all made up, your old straight face
painted the way you never could abide.
Young Clive said, 'That's not Grandma.' This set Mum,
who never cried much, crying. When we'd stripped
your bed, we carried it upstairs, a swap
for my old lumpy one. And the commode
went uphill too, in case, you never knew.
The kitchen stretched out like a new-lined pitch.

The Woods

My mother's siblings - not a word she'd use –
lived in still terraces of monochrome
with shadowy back-yards, front-gardens
where they grew tea-cups, sponge-cakes, trifles,
red salmon sandwiches and never moved
more than a street or two, unless they married
into a different album on the shelf,
dusty with coal and thick with cotton fluff.
They went to work and war, back to their house,
visited family and had family visit,
the kitchen full of women washing up,
the kitchen table giving kids house room,
while men played boredom with the clock that sat
on every mantelpiece and tocked and ticked
existence off while none of them were looking.
Before that, they'd creaked each night up wooden hills
and must have moved there sometimes to ward off
the upstairs chill and damp, to lift the weight
of eiderdown and blankets, must have moved
as I have cousins who are living proof,
a nurse, a printer, estate agent's clerk,
amateur twitcher, and a mayor of Rochdale.
All of us keep dead parents somewhere safe -
an attic or a cellar we don't use,
a cupboard under stairs, a cardboard suitcase -
where they can sit and goggle at the box,
wear Whitsun best, share a nice pot of tea
and never have to stir to see to us
or put coal on the fire. I visit them,
and all look ready for a good night's rest.

In her print pinnie, size of a scout tent,
Lizzie who lives up to her rhyme and keeps
both church and vicarage clean, makes Allen smile,
serious Allen, Leather wed to Wood.
Marie has flowery blouses and loud hats
and seems to keep her Ken moth-balled and pressed,
on a coat-hanger, ready when required.
Albert the gas man wears his uniform,
he has kind eyes that swirl in the thick swim
of marbled lenses that he glimpsed us through.
Harry wed Alice, lives next to the cut,
their street is shadowed by the spinning mill.
Herbert died 1900, nine months old,
and Margaret, leaving one girl, three boys,
at 39, when I was only two.
John (Jack), the youngest and the last to die,
lived happy in a heap of laughing kids
we gave up counting, he'd turned Catholic
for Edna, never regretted it, shows me
her photos, shy as if just engaged,
when he is eighty and has months to live
before their heavenly wedding date is fixed.
Nellie was first of ten and had to mother,
when mother died months after Jack was born,
the youngest kids. She stayed kind to the end.
At Blackpool once with us her veins required
a rest, her and mum sharing an ornate seat
along the prom with some young couple.
She thanked them for the treat as we walked on.
And there is Joe, his arm, the wooden one
he got as stand-by for the one he'd left
in France. Too young to fight, he lied and went.

The doctor said he broke his mother's heart,
this soldier boy sent home, no further use.
He does not use the arm, it stays behind
a curtain by the door. I never asked,
will not get round to asking cousins now
who've spread themselves and little images
out over England, scattered like the sand
from Southport in a wild southwesterly,
the arm's last resting place. Did it burn in fire
or does it rot in earth like all the Woods,
Nancy, her siblings? Not a word she'd use.

The Superintendent

Freddie Bramwell: that to your face not one
of us would ever have dared call you
or even thought to breathe out such a note
of disrespect into the smoke-tattoo

that tanned your well-creased hide, Rev. F.T.B.
Cloth of your calling, given better weather,
would have sprouted baccy's huge greens
from its dark soils. But this was Lancashire,

coal, cotton, cables and the big, cold manse
triple-mounted with its red-brick, soot-stained
wall, black railings, gloomy laurels stiff
as my grandma's rheumatics when it rained.

Grammar school boy who, like you, read books,
you gave me time like there was no life after,
paid visits to our Martha and then talked
over her and teacups about literature.

You said nothing would please you more than me
being a minister, preaching the word
like you. But just one thing, if that call came
I should run off, defy it, wrestle hard,

wriggle out. Only if, pinned to God's earth,
I'd no escape, should I accept relief
from doubt. It was the worst job in the world
when turned to dust, despair and disbelief.

So now I wonder how you'd reconciled
your passions with the collar, only guess
the secret lay in those long Sunday sermons.
Performance artist of the word made flesh,

I loved your show, hung on your argument
from dark to bright, firebranding rhetoric,
tried pulpits on myself for fit, despite
your excellent advice to beat it quick.

You talked me into Iris Murdoch
just then come out in Penguin, half a crown,
and brought the stationer's to a dumbstruck stop
by ordering *Lady Chatterley*, first in town.

Your morning studies, sacred and profane,
stoked up your faith with strong St. Bruno's aid,
while Wesleyans in want of pentecosts
warmed to the tongue that licked across their heads.

I left to study English, you retired to read.

Conspiratorial

for my mother

That morning, bare light will shake me,
crack each eye open like an egg,
start with its jumpy wires
my raw feet twitching, singe
my temples, dangle and dance me.

That morning, I will not know your name,
I will know nothing about you,
not your face, your identifying marks,
not the scar above your groin,
not one syllable I will tell, the truth.

That morning, the cosh of ignorance,
the sharp stick of denial
will pulp your bed to innocence,
a white-out, an absolution
on the ward's safe confessional.

That morning, you can tell me
where you will hide the body.
It is what I have. The loss like all loss
is required. *Hold on!* or something
you hiss, a cobra, a bronco.

That morning, here are its contents:
an arm's jerked jump the prayer,
the lock of hair a holy fragment,
closeness of smell that passes understanding
and your eye an empty tomb.

That morning, late or early
I'll be off somewhere. When they find me,
I will drive five hours into your night
waiting for me, our holding on.
All that long morning. They will never catch you.

Souvenirs

Right at the back of the wardrobe
Time I had a clear out
Heaps of old programmes.

Lost games with dead players
Somebody got fed up of them
Gave them to a nine year old.

He is 35 and lives in New York
With no space for souvenirs
So they have shared our house.

Can't bag them with today's paper
I stack them in a sort of order
The Boro, United, England, The Rest.

When I'm certified immortal
The kids won't have room for all this
Shall we chuck these or do you want them?

We all have this ghost in the spare room
It can't remember who it played for
But its dream goals duster the shelves.

A Place to Write

Under windows of shovelled sky, cloud stones,
under ceilings levelled with sun, lifted with rain,
I sit between air and earth, I scribble down
through floor-boards cracked with silence,
worm through books of soil. I squeeze my words

in this abandoned seam: water, foul air, roof-fall
prise workings open, undermine the house.
His pit-prop name scratches my retina: John Wood,
my mother's father, hewer of that coal,
who came up every shift, died in the light.

He goes back down, weighed deeper now
in the ply of family, layers of generation,
by his child's eighty heavy years,
my mother, Nancy, pitman's daughter
who has died in the pitmen's hospital.

His pick's turned marble, it taps out in me,
on this thin paper, at the shivered membrane.
He chips the words of bone, such imaginings
in tunnels low, hot, deep, confined.
A man could only crawl and not turn.

At last I am listening, there is a line
formed, their desires bursting up and out
in the ancestral queue, the breath fractured,
the languages bubble hot like springs of mud,
at last someone is listening, who should write it down.

But they must wait their turn, the last come first.
My mother is not ready yet to speak to me
and turns me back from all of them gone dead.
She leaves me with the living, with the season
this place to write, surfaces not shored up.

Winter Breaks – poems from the sequence

2. Severe
Why should they mind my cuts and bruises?
Their child is now a wealthy bride.

An insane howl somewhere behind the gas fire,
autumnal from the south west, gives me notice,
the topsy-turvied earth launches its offensive,
minded to wipe me clean from its once smiling
     surface.

What happens as you get older is not just
balding head, hairy ears, the thickened toe-nails
you learn to lie with, but disenchantment severing
dreams, intentions in slices, feeding them to the gale.

Nobody gives a piss, registers a thing
some nursing home can't cure; they get wed, insured,
childed, no point telling the flattened aftermath.
In silence this sightless stuff must be heard out,
     endured.

6. Restoration

with feet that drag me down,
through life that's bright and happy

A sky stuffed with light, the North Sea flattened
under off-shore wind, gusts steer me and suck
      sideways,
concessionary tripper to this war zone,
sheep grazing the cavities, all that is carious.

For us there is nothing to do out here but rot,
the bony curtain wall, the slackening teeth.
Bright plastic bottles keep their colour up,
carry it off every storm, top the fringe of wrack.

Across old landfalls jets scud low, invade
our failing hearing, lock on crumbling towers.
Flower-lists in churches allocate a future,
gulls hang on up there, shriek to the last herring.

Time drags more-often-stumbling legs along
the shifty edge of wet and dry, I tell myself,
don't be so bloody miserable, a great day out
ends well with crab and pint in the hostelry.

It's *The Jolly Fisherman*, so all aboard.
The dead raise glasses to the waiting ocean,
drink to their winter breaks, fish bones up from the
      soup.
Boat people drown out there to join these classes.

9. Recall

How differently you made me welcome,
you fickle and inconstant town!
Lark, nightingale, each lit your windows
and strove to sing the other down.

Remembering the exact spot where
this happened or, if not this, that,
is harder than it appeared in first light
stamping approval on desired, then handheld beauty
as I did yours and do recall the light or rather
the flesh on which it fell or into which its fill
cascaded, but not the number or the street at all.
To say this is not to say it was done casually.

Returning now would be to pull down, tear
the fabric of the old and rotten curtain
I've patched up against birdsong and the dawn,
their treacherous disposition to be sunny
as my first falling in was, seems still so
where it has gone. An old mind plays tricks, games
and with itself, no choice, those sodden dreams
through which breath creaks, pulse coughs, heart
   staggers flimsy.

10. Notice

And when the cocks crowed early,
my heart was wakened wide

Off for the winter, are you? Bloody hell!
And with old you-know-who along as well?
No need to add explanatory text,
just leave me wondering what you'll tell me next!

Not that I've ever fancied winter sports,
the snazzy awful clothes, the grim reports
of avalanches, all that après-ski,
this is the stuff brings out the worst in me,

the opposite of all the things you like.
When fear kicks in, the nice parts go on strike,
you told me what they were once, can't recall,
but winter sports craps white-out on them all.

You look as if to say you'd thought I might
go thick-eyed as a damp November night
and typically forget to think that spring
will come and you with it, appearing

like what's-her-name from out the underworld,
your face all sun-tanned and your legs unfurled.
I don't forget. If looks could resurrect,
I'd melt the sodden lot, leave winter wrecked,

have all its sports slopped soggy down the drain,
so I could live full-time with you again
in light and warm and dry, not give a shit
what happened to the global warming bit.

You could snap back there never was a time
when we had that arrangement, but your rhyme
to my disgruntlement's infantile myth
is softer, subtler, telling me the truth

and that it's seasonal, its ebbs and flows,
synapses, snaps, stanzaic body-blows
are hymns to love, antiphonal, at odds
with what we dream of snatching from the gods.

As usual, you'll persuade me that's the way,
I'll start the countdown day by bloody day,
hoping next spring and summer lie ahead,
knowing each one is one less till we're dead.

12. Circular
The post brings none to you addressed

That morning was so dark, it made me shift
to raise the blind, it was the sky. So far
so good, and then they dropped with dead flies' drift
through the door's slot, first shots of festive fare
from friends who scratch my grudges every year.

Don't need to open them, watch it go by
the weather out there, listen to the clock
cough, you know their parents died or will die
soon enough, or they've split up, but will attack
once more their wed address list, sound heroic.

My age and literate, what's to be done?
Let them write out last year's disaster list
and demonstrate how we must cope and grin
when genius kids are middle-aging fast,
poor specimens of what the future's passed.

They're managing, not companies or gangs,
but getting by, and they are keeping jolly
as muscle shrinks, as joints give out, most things
work with a something aid, and gradually
plastic and steel replace the flesh's folly.

Their celebration is that they survive
and I'm supposed to raise my glass to that,
treasure their trips in photographic trove,
sundown safari or the cruise round Crete.
You have to see the sunny side of fate,

I guess, to be a golfer, bash your balls
across some crimplene cow-cleared meadowland,
or go to adult ed., sit in cold halls,
empty your flask while cluttering your mind
with stuff the temporary staff don't understand.

If, it's not likely, any of them read this
and take offence at my ingratitude,
they might feel I am extracting the piss,
finding their kind intentions misconstrued.
My lifelong learning is in being rude.

Putting it blunt, a card will do next time,
merry old mash, happy new mish, such shlock,
which is all that I need to hear from them
on the other side. It's a piece of cake,
a candle, somebody there when I knock..

13. Freeze

Snow, you know all my desires:
Now where do you want to go?

Think of yourself as a glacier by all means, the progeny
of deep winter, will give a reassurance in the coldness,
the solidity, the hands-off-me slippiness of surface.
You will not though be able to deny that there is
    movement

and that it is towards me, inevitable, the ice's pull
downhill, out from the cold core, to where it finds
    some warmth,
and that this movement at its adventurous extremity
melts to a flow that is simply water and feeds
    springtime.

Not so simple. If the earth is cracked in the head,
    infected
or insane, poisoned, made war on, if it's in raging fever,
what can save you from liquidity, from the
    defencelessness,
the wetness of love? Or rescue me from the weight
    of such tears?

Trying too hard. Only a lump of flesh that's past its
    freshest,
that grows chill across the shoulders, at the softness
    of the back,
as in a damp night late in my years I write and
    cannot know
what gets by through thin air to where you may not
    feel the cold

or where you sit inside the mind of a new house,
    whether you
are making order of so much snow, packing it into
    chests,
loading the shelves with it, reading its not-to-be-
    deciphered sounds
or playing them on refrigerators, the silent white keys.

15. Collection

Joy and sadness, all our caring,
are this light's misleading game.

The light's eternal, so I'm done, that's it,
locked into holy day, its collection box,
a roof of angels that mum lullabies.

Up through the slot, against the drip of pence,
I shove this out on an old biro, it's
my last communiqué on my last ten quid.

So, if you want, see the light, be born again,
just forget anything I felt or said
for you, to you, and get rid of the tapes.

All the moaning and groaning we did,
blew it on the wrong horse, liked its name and
no more waste of time than all the rest.

You could get your revenge, you could curse
some god for my metamorphosis, small change,
join in the hymns or pull the temple down.

But I'd rather you left me quick and ran
back into the dark, love, of primroses,
might be a few left, before the bright sky drops.

16. Accommodation

Are all the rooms in this house
already occupied?

Another wintry visit to the Crem,
increasingly those late night phone calls come
with their reminders: life is but a dream,
morning no more than *in memoriam*.

It's rather like the Post House down the road,
same bricks, same shrubs and lawns, same
    chimney stack.
I wonder if they offer bed and board,
ask at the desk, but no-one answers back.

Now I am envying (you as well?) the sod
who's made it to the safety of the casket
and wishing it was me up there instead,
the Roller, silk sheets, chicken in the basket.

No Vacancies and not *Abide with me*
the tape's repeating on the life machine.
Don't hang about, piss off and get your tea,
you're at death's door though, keep your knickers
    clean.

19. Waiting

so that I hate my youth's long day –
the grave's rest still so far!

Late January, under the church wall's height
the snowdrops struggle out, their papery white
as sparse and pale as hairs left in my head.
Their anchors are the chalked lines of the dead.

The year that's gone, so far from what we guessed,
the worst much worse, the good far from the best,
the new graves not those that we had predicted,
our choice of plot by these that much restricted.

Now, as the footpaths open up and stick
swings round and thwacks to raise the bramble's sneck,
the gales sweep in and turn the fields to flood,
the resurrected sheep are fleeced in mud.

These summaries of day in winter's long
and whining *tenebrae*, that lights-out song,
these snowdrops rise, their paper white as bone,
brief IOUs, on which I could write down

the debts I owe you, love, this time of year
when hope and joy get trampled under fear,
attraction shrinks all shrivelled in the cold
and passion hugs its blanket damp with mould.

The dead beat grasses lying in my way
will lift their seed-heads to the longest day,
so everything will come to one who waits
with fading snowdrops by the churchyard gates.

20. Rambler

My heart sees in the heavens
its picture painted bold –
it's nothing else but winter,
a winter wild and cold!

Go walking where you'll meet no bugger else,
get up them hills, let winds of winter bray
each inch of skin, of flesh, of skeleton
and whittle eyes down onto *imago*.

Project your heart's bleeding content out
on that blockbuster sky, don't give a sod –
burnt bracken's casting couch lacks an incumbent,
like bed back home it's damp, cold, empty, hard.

Spoil-heaps and their old mines are such refusals
as grow you lumps, subside you, shaft your throat;
plantation conifers stride down the fellside,
skin-prickling dreams, you shiver, want to shit.

The sun has turned its arse, pale as a camp child,
on death's rollover total, flaunts its moons
brightblinding fence-posts, can't help but remind
you're the remainder of these long divisions:

last human on the shelf of winter's planet,
one writer-reader, *poeta ergo sum*.
Convivial as wanking, hopeful as a sperm bank,
when you feel bad, up here's the place you'll come.

23. Love Song

before this, walking kept me cheered,
the barren tracks my testing.

When you keep going you keep going.
I'm telling you. I'm telling you
you keep going you stay warm.
When you're managing you keep moving.

When you change it you stay alive
you're moving you're staying warm.
You remind me I forget that
you are managing, keeping going.

When you mind it you stay warm.
I'm telling you, I'm telling you
when you keep going you keep going,
staying alive, keep it moving.

I remind you. You forget that
if you're moving you're staying warm.
When you manage it you keep moving,
staying alive and keep it changing.

When you're managing you keep warm.
I'm telling you, I'm telling you.
You stay alive, you keep going,
you're moving, it's forgetting.

You stop changing, you get moved.
You're reminding to keep forgetting.
You stop moving, you get cold.
I'm telling you, you stay going.

I forget who. You remind me
when you're going you keep moving.
Stop the changing, staying tired of,
getting minded, can't be managing.

You stop living, you stay dead.
Are you minding, are you telling me
you forget how? I'm getting to.
Can't be changing what's reminding.

You're done to, you're changed past,
you're moved by, you're cold down,
I mind when, alive who,
staying gone, I am telling you.

Viewer

News item: In the States there are now more pornographic video shops than there are McDonalds restaurants.

My father was a stud in hardcore film,
His crotch full as a sail, well hung
Between strong masts. He took the helm,
Could pilot weaker vessels with his tongue.

An expert. He applied his country craft,
Fixing each piece of earth with his ploughshare
That furrowed deep. Dust, breaking on his shaft,
Lifted its treasure to the sky's bright stare.

Reined mares, the sweating flanks rolled round
And back into the soil. His eye
Narrowed, long lens angled. In he ground,
Coming on cue, in line, exactly.

I wanted to grow up and plough,
To close one eye, stiffen my sex.
But all I did was watch him. How
His pale flesh banged on who came next.

I tripped and fell upon his stallion's work.
His dying whinnies filled that autumn day.
He left me only all this thrust and jerk,
The harnessed, harrowed ghosts I play and play.

Reading Your Spine

as night and daylight turn
fonts of skin, faded erasures,
bones' braille, each coiled crux.

I excavate the down of script,
I can't disturb your sleep
with my soft scrape of verse.

You'd closed the book, you'd slipped
through the unlettered door,
you'd gone down silent

to the obscure depths
I can't reach, can't make out,
all that's authorial.

Text you would proof in the glass,
illustrate as you dressed,
teach me by heart,

it's at my fingertips.
If you were to open again
on the tender stalks of my eyes.

Tomb Decoration: Cattle

Not a breath. It was the painter's rod
froze these waves hard,
assault-craft beefing up the last resort,
a troupe lifting repeated legs all down the line,
skimming a cresty froth from the pigments' tide.
Their cloned accompaniment beyond decay
mimes *Moo-mummify-me,*
they promenade the years to here.

Goggle at the symmetry of this chorus,
admire the delicate boy, his arm
signing them forward, young god of the surf.
He carries rope in a coil, the star of the show,
the hangman, the saviour who can light the fuse,
set the spangled heap to bonfire.

We can't expect them just to swagger on,
hot rasps from nose and throat,
the hitch up of a tail, a flood
of steamy piss or runny shit,
the hustling of flies around an ear,
the glitter that stirks' eyes are brainy with.

But here they come again
stitching their final sequence in reverse,
shuffling it subtly so it's hardly noticed.
They'll not miss a good funeral,
hoofing it two soft shoes at a time
up the steep dive of the escalator.

All that rehearsal for
the silent months of quarantine.
Their eyes fill with the indifference
cows practise when their calves are taken
and they swell with milk, make statues
in the dusky grass at long past milking.

Song for Mario

More than an island
you were learning to sail
on those choppy words
a little boat to
maybe, one day, Chile.

And into your being,
lover, communist, martyr, poet.
You found your silence, you sang it
under boots, under truncheons.
The redness inside you, outside you.

The damage of poems
that change the impossible.
Is the whole world a metaphor?
you asked that poet.
A circle on a blank page.

There it goes, small white ball,
riots through all the defence.
Your woman's mouth secretes it,
your son's hand holds it.
Little white ball of earth
shoots the circumference.

And there you go,
almost silent fish,
escaping the sad nets
with the tide's blood.
Maybe, one day, Chile.

In the Purse

I lost it years ago and never guessed
it slipped straight down between the lining
and the leather, lay there flat and stiff
as kids in long grass, playing dead.

I tired of looking for it, thought it best
obliterated with one wipe. I watched
the dust put coats on sills, on lintels, breath
that counted to ten thousand while you hid.

Ready or not. Up cracked stairs. Our almost
empty room. One cupboard jammed with damp.
Inside it, swaddled in that moth-chewed fur
your mother wanted me to wear (I never did),

the purse I carried when we wed. I twist
the rusted clasp, let fingers in again,
follow them down into the frayed silk seams
and find it, sick of being sought, not glad

to have its boniness fished out at last,
a grey-faced relic from its shabby shrine,
lining and leather. Love, is that all it was,
your name on it, and all I ever had?

Manhattan Piece

After midnight, a one-way,
rain hosing brake-lights
into the gutters, legless,
squealing, a blaze of eyes.

Inching between
parked metal-shine,
moving metal-shine.
WALK / DON'T WALK
he is doing both.

Has the ripped umbrella up,
a bag full of stuff,
coat without buttons,
rest too dark to see
but the cardboard square
at his chest wet through.

He walks / does not walk
into the darkness,
swirls of rain, electric red.
The numbered streets
lead all ways to deep water.
The city pumps in neon blood.

Has the face of a hero,
broken stone, grimed stone,
face like a lost star.
That flickering, patient sky.
Insect aircraft pinned up there
offering the sacraments.

The Afternoon Slot

Post-Impressionism, Middlesbrough
reads the label on the box, it is one
of six dun-cow-discoloured boxes stacked
beneath the radiator, draped with coats
we dropped with bags that spill their papers out.
The other boxes' labels too far off
to read in lecture room, this adult class
writing out solitary sentences.

Writing out solitary sentences
serves as a seventh box of sorts, it lacks
the alloy handles, rivets down each edge,
cupped corners, reinforcing strips.
The table shivers to pen-pushing time,
the tutor scatters carpet's bleary blue
with photographs of gravestones by the yard,
of mausolea and of cenotaphs.

Of mausolea and of cenotaphs,
a monochrome confetti-fall of ash,
we could soon get sick. Who's it for, this box?
What might be mouldering away in there?
A plant about to go critical with
an after-life we must prick out in verse,
so aching long to learn post-kingdom-come?
Endeavour and Discovery, lift the lid.

Endeavour and discovery lift the lid
expecting brushes, oils, intense sensation,
sharp palette knife, *la vie*, a roseate

pointilliste impressioning - but we find,
corrected, Teesside colour proofs, the prints
of post-industrial green fields, remains
of charnel towers that swallowed fire and sky:
Post-Impressionism, Middlesbrough.

Early June 2003, Grandchildren

Sunday afternoon. Not one snip of cloud.
The mouse in the kitchen skirting
recumbent for its final siesta.
Next door the TV talks in its sleep,
too fast, it gives the game away,
the Grand Prix racing, Eurosport,
the calculating whine, the cicadas
corporate and circling. Sky,
getting warm, so Spain, somewhere close
where life goes extending the airport,
the flyovers, the centre of nations.
Pulling tight the belt: *residencia,*
barrio commercial, condominio.
And any day now our second grandchild
on cue for crowd scenes, the cast of thousands
in the heavy wings of her waiting.

Two-year-old hand and voice signal 'plane'
up in a sort of heaven and we say 'yes',
do not pull him from the terrace
or force him three steps at a time
into the basement's chill.
We sit tight over dinner, look where
only the darkness falls
on the capital streets. Below us
the trains run clean and regular, white rats.
Perched in their orthodontic grins
the oldest *paisanos*, suckled when bombs
outnumbered rains and the fields
let burn, left uncut. They smile up

small and contentedly at their teenagers,
admire the scaffold-work of two generations.

So come and be about it, little one,
before the hottest of days hit town.
Who knows what we make of each other
or say when it's our lines to speak,
madrileña and you, her Manhattan brother?

Beethoven Back of Blencarn

jostles the dark, elbows the
dirty-windowed road
aside, pulls two rabbits
out of its hedges
and over its ears.

You rabbits, you two
fur-lined stiffies
in the full-beam frazzle
defrosting those lollopy legs
will you just
stagger it staccato it
hop it to the verge and
melt into the dark
spare me the dazzle.

I'm in a fierce noisy starship
I'm staring in the uncertain
I'm swooping the blinded road
I'm a-hunting a-kenning a-peeling-off
the pity and illumination.

Here's speaker-spitting applause
here's two rabbits
between road edges
between galaxies
here's my fingers hung
on the whirly wheel
my eyes shrinking and swelling
here's a torchlight of questions

here's a terror of bright
here's my ears slinking
in the skulk hole of a dead man
the skull hulk of a deaf man

who is jostling again
always elbowing
into the major
telling me to listen
as if he knows the way
beyond the throw of the light.

The Price You Pay

I was cycling to the rainbow,
the near end, one tree more luminous
than the rest, that copse six long fields off.

Every road was a trough, a wash, a this-is-
what-happens when the tears flow,
a tyre-to-mudguard swish of sorrows, sorrows.

And I was asking for that trouble, good grief
cycling to the rainbow where it leapt
between the darks of cloud cliff and fellside.

Round Culgaith, a man on the back lane,
a man with five spaniels leashed out in a spray.
It's the price you pay for rainbows, I told him.

Now, after Skirwith, Ousby, fourteen miles,
all of it poured over, and me dry-skating through
puddles of shiny sky, the clean blue cheek of it.

Trees shaking wet green fleeces, they pelt their
hand-me-downpours at anyone passing,
still miss me, parched as a proper summer.

The last few yards, unmade, uphill, are not impressed
and ditch me sideways. The bike scrapes four cog-teeth
in bloody parallels above the hoof. To teach me.

But it won't. Not yet. A rainbow on two wheels,
of course which can't exist. While it does,
ride the impossible, breathable, proof.

At St. Leonard's

i.m. Roger Kirk, York, January 2003

Visiting you the last time
in the low slant of daylight
I met you lying at the sun's edge
where you could see the funny side
and haul yourself onto it
when your back got weary
of the serious business
with its indoors and ceilings.

So you did, you turned
to watch a solemn comedy,
me dropping your catch of words
unruly syllables we could not get in line.

Then taking me unawares
you stretched your hand to my face
fastened your fingers on my nose
wagged it so curiously
from side to side.

Perhaps it was a thing
you had wanted to do
years ago, one of those meetings
in your office, instead of coffee,
or over dinner, generous host,
to substitute a second glass.
But what you told me
smiling as you bent it
I lacked the language for
sensing some honour in this tender mischief.

And now you are still.
Spring in your garden
will grow full of your wisdom.
Birds will nest in its hedgerow
bulbs burn with its energy.
It was always the young
you worked for, the future
you spoke to, the light
you understood as everlasting.

I should think of you in terms
of courage, of a kind gentleness
but that's not the way of it
when a good man's died.
You'd tweak me for abstraction.
I'll remember the first flower
of the year you had lived to see
brought by love from home.
There in a little glass, bright beside you.
Or sometimes in the mirror
I'll give my rubbery nose a twist or two,
recall your enigmatic punch-line
and wonder, when I catch you up,
if I'll have got the joke.

No Ice

for John Macleod

Glenlivet 12, cheers,
no water thanks, no ice.
There's just me in the bar,
I don't ask twice.
The barman knows my taste
and fills my glass
without a second glance
to make this long night pass.
The others left the warmth,
the light, my company
on some wild goose hunt
for divinity.

Some new-born baby
in the pub-yard shed,
I don't know yet
if it's alive or dead
or what on God's earth
it is doing there
with two dead tractors
and a cracked-up chair.

They soon come back,
they're shivering with cold,
then by the open fire
the tale gets told.
I hear the yearly nonsense
about stars and sheep,
voices from up the sky,
it makes a wise man weep.

They do still look amazed
and they are really nice
to everyone. Won't last,
I get my order in, precise:
Glenlivet 12, cheers,
no water thanks, no ice.

Calvary

In this oak screen there's symmetry at least,
the windowed sun cross-membered by a Christ,
his face rubbed almost featureless.

Framework and trunk of this earth's map:
the head set north, feet nailed to south;
arms in their soft ellipses
stretch fingers east and west.

Each pane mirrors across. Above
two angels comfort or two devils taunt.
Both lean one elbow on the crucifix,
both stretch their tongue-curled wings,
both set a footprint on one chiselled wrist.

Two sharp-nosed pikemen, sure of their place beneath,
align their shafts, south-east, south-west,
in with the grain of flesh. One constant point
is sealed inside the God below the ribs;
the second lifts a bitter sponge, oak-gall.

The maker's skilled hands raised all this
to the light and have let no-one leave
to flit to heaven or hell, to march
back into barracks and a night of wine.

Till this world burns and falls, they'll watch
that worn-down face, hear nothing from
the never-opened, slowly erasing lips.

The Man in the Pub Said

You see it more as you get old and stale
when memory's the dog and life the tail.

You see much clearer how it is, the norm
as death comes closer, rigour getting warm.

Stark as a streaker, factual as a fuck,
there's no denying it, no nip and tuck

can pluck it from the flesh, exit its grip,
no way you can jam-then-unjam its zip.

Your vision's tested, two dead rings for Dante,
straight as a Boro street, taut as a twisted panty,

as finely focused as a photo shoot,
sharper than any Moss Bros wedding suit.

Ruder than rude health, brassier than brass,
sharp and as splintered as a fist of glass:

your generation's risen, falls like grass
and like the rest you'll end tip under ass.

February

The young year's bent already with our sorrows,
manna of winter, startled whites of eyes.
A god giving bread can terrify.
The indifferent mercy of weather
showing its pale hand, saying 'Who?'
I don't know in truth, but it will melt
in its own mouth the fragile crystals
so crocodiles of tears will jam the becks,
rip chops off the leathery fells.

Grains of ice bounce on sandstone flags,
robin, wren, blackbird beak and claw
the peanut scraps shot down from aerial devilment,
that squadron screech of blue tits fighting
for all our lives through the bright flak.

Remains

Wind, wet and white stuff
flattened the roadside grass.
This skeleton's unstitched, picked clean
so disassembled pelvis, scapulae, the rest
signal the compass points
on rusty green, rough of an old man's chin.

A week after snowfall the bones of it
anatomise the fell with dazzling lines of wall,
in drifted ossuaries down miry pits.
Shorn early of its storm-proof coat
this upland ewe, broad-backed,
shivers for birth and its crumb of summer.

I set the delicately nosing skull
as lookout on an edge of stone:
one pale card played
on stacks of blood-red tropic sand
a million icy winters steadied down.

Old Friend

Good morning. So another day. We'll take it.
Temperate with a light wind
teasing the skeins of cloud across the sun.

You've got to grips with my dark-humoured fun
and come to understand that what's beneath's
a sense, in every thing's delight, in ours,

of its sweet brevity. My dad, two years
my senior, might have glimpsed
that sooty nonconformist flare

but never was allowed to get that near,
barred by his wanting me to be the best,
the most he then could never make.

Mum used to say 'For heaven's sake'
hoping we'd just be happy, fit and fed.
She got through life never expecting much

but you have got a different touch,
accepting stoic, striving epicure,
young in the sixties, in your sixties young,

responding newborn as a Schubert song
to every pleasure, every injury.
From you I've learned to open up my heart,

managed to slow my slide into old fart,
to celebrate the better, weigh the worse
as with the kids whose photographs we show,

bright upstarts who already know,
as grandchildren will soon, we got it wrong
and they can do things better come what may.

For me and you is what remains to say
when luck has brought us here for one more day:
Good morning. Weather, daylight, us. We'll take it.

Lost Child

You were never a lost child,
always you held your hand
out to my hold. Smiled always
when I wrapped it round.

Never a lost child. You were
here all the day. All the night
you lay in your deep bed, floated
through walls into dreams.

Lost, you were never
a lost child, were you?
Fact is that I'll be one.
Gone away, the street all empty.

You will call me, call me.
To tea, to my favourite programme.
Bedtime. I still won't come. Never.
Again and again. A lost child.

Old Wolves

He woan't be baack for maany a year
So sheeep, sheeep, come out of theer

as Granddad Wolf sneaked in from Manchester
on the Number 26, snarkled past chapel and basket
    works,
used special key, slithered his scratchy claws
through shop, behind the counter, into the kitchen
and opened wide his mouth and eyes of Grandson
    Sheep,
me, who got out of theer and hid behind the sofa
or the pantry curtain. How they laughed
    afterwards,
lamb, really, and rheumatic, dentured wolf, whose
    jaws
grinned all night by the sink, in a chipped mug.

Now I am old, I get the canine part. A threat
to fleecy grandchildren, I send them scattering
through larger rooms, round backs of smarter
    furniture.
Now I know the trick, never to go to Manchester
but lurk, pretend a pensioner's ferocity.
Slyly I put on wolfskin, top hat, silk gloves,
white-spots-on-crimson pocket handkercher,
could pass quite unremarked across St. Peter's
    Square.
The mirror in the hall – ooh look at you now,
if it's not Granddad Wolf, to the life, back from the
    dead
of understairs. Not easy to shrug off.

In there the lambs are dancing in the light
waiting which door will open. I tell my old man in
    the glass,
my cue. He nods and will come too, the game's
    duplicitous.
We are and so are they, can play their parts. They
    run the show,
plot their determination, audition for the cast, treat me
as firm as Peter Quince would Bottom. So today
I'm a good wolf and must negotiate when bad ones
    come
to snatch my little deer from their frail house.
I hurl spells, utter threats, seduce with plastic burgers.
But in they tramp again, this time, I'm told,
their king leading the pack. Flashing his teeth and tie.

Beyond the wisdom of grandfathers, past the
    experience
of reformed carnivores who play at bites and snarls,
whose scratch is ticklish. The king of the bad
    wolves,
that war-crime-splattered general, defies us all.
Good, good-for-not-much wolf tells useless truth,
    I don't
know what to do. But four-years piglet does, will twirl
this story's devil by its bushed-out tail.
Tells me – Don't worry, Grandpa, it will be OK,
I will be Spiderman, you will be Batman, we will
    beat them.
As at last we do - with leaps and bounds, in
expelled breaths,
by sharp karate chops. This once his generation is
    secured.

And mine - like any wolf with eyes long weighed
    with ice
or grandparent blessed with time's miracle,
our helpless babies grown to fullness, fuller still,
themselves the parents of these new-born lambs
that leap and totter – my generation starts its
    shrivelling,
its shadow tracing out from Manchester
across the web of airlines' arcing paths. There's one
lifts me from memory to Madrid, September,
    afternoon
where grandson gives this master-class for me,
the high-kick dance, the bonehouse-shattering cry.
Old wolves can learn new tricks, so young beasts
    thrive.

Equinoctial

For Ellie, 29 March 2006

Wind from the south west bearing rain
on its warm air; birds in the garden
clamour in mating, most coupled, some still
unsolved in tag-wrestle threesomes.

We are waiting on time as our lives all do,
on the light's turn, a birth, some celebration
of acknowledgement. The gusts tug at our house
and lay daffodil heads, chase old leaves and
    wrappers.

These least, like your primed cards in their packs,
try on a bright dress, as one sliver of sun
glosses puddles. The odds stack for localised
    flooding,
not here though, east of Pennine embankments.

West of that watershed, becks add to rivers
carving again in Lune's snare-shifty sandflats
the names of the drowned that might sound so alike,
who now only wait with each tide in its coming

and bend with the moon through its barren seasons.
Here to the east, the older folk sleeping and just
before dawn, a flooding of life under night's hard
    stare.
Your child's born, sweet as air, sweet as rain, as
    spring.

Uncollected Poem

Published in *Night Balancing,*
Blinking Eye Publishers 2006.

Terminal

We'd have said 'Millionaire's Row',
one of many, row on gated row,
flatly insisting they can't recall
the headlong-pouring terraces
up sodden Pennine valleys.

Heathrow they coin it,
taste on flotsam breath
its frothy race, diesel, kerosene,
to turn the stones, to grind
our offspring-upstarts into gold.
Fruit-machine's retched-up roar
deafening sheds of looms
into their lip-read silence.
Easy how silver shuttles
sing through deep sky
spooling a mill town's worth of souls
by the doors of heaven.

Each revolution makes,
must break, its promises.
One more parched winter here,
these licks of reservoirs,
where Thames will rip
in upstream spate
reaping a late return

on gardens and avenues;
cerulean pools, until they silt,
drag in the drift of patios.
Bird-tables, suicides, bankrupt stock.

Today sun shines, hail stones.
We match our kinder-tennis
to a shirtsleevish February.
Alice at not-yet-three
lifts up her eyes unto
each groaning, winged
arrival in the stack.

FROM *STILL LIFE* 2012

This Bed

This bed is the bed of dreams, they all start
from this bed, a white hole swallowing
the collapsing star. They pulverise memory,
compound my tenses in a nightmare play.

This bed flies over the realities of day,
it ignores the world's exploding cries,
bedsides of sighs, of soft expiries,
the molten craters of birth.

This bed and me, we hovercraft,
we swish our skirts across
too numerous, too predictable agonies.
And you think I should care for them?

Even this bed sobs, gutters groan with tears,
the world a flash flood, cars elbowing bridges.
And tomorrow will bear down heavier,
will bend the earth's back.

We lie in wait for it, watching the sky,
never knowing what we must muddle through,
this night's throw of the diazepam dice.
As if, this bed and me, we were life's burden.

And down below us, sufferers making moan,
I hope you will sleep, every last one,
quiet and deep as the many dead,
with never a swift or little owl to wake you.

Man Writing an E-mail with his Carer

My room's at the end of the wing in the unit,
hers indeterminate, its window to the east.
Easy to move from here to the imagined there
of this postcard, from TV's clapping-happy hymn
through the wall, as deaf as any gospel choir
to argument, move to where she bends,
ink almost dry on her last word. That sideways light,
the chequerboard tiles, and hung behind her table
the dusky painting, its darkening oils.
The blackened frame bisects her world
between the fixed old dispensation
and shifting new, where paint is not quite dry,
anything could move, the dark fold in a skirt,
that cambric sleeve, a delicate lace cap.

The darkness is my hide, the sun out there
catches its fiery breath. My lines on screen
thicken and thin in crystal mist, carers change shifts
and busy in with medication, cups of tea, snatch glances
at summer through the glass, talk of a lottery win.
Pale wraiths of women lift the infant Moses,
Pharaoh's daughter, handmaidens, his deceiving mother.
There is the beginning of something,
a shiver in the gauze curtain, shadow of air,
the pale geometries of the window glass,
the maid at the still centre, arms crossed,
her gaze subdued, whatever stirs out there.
The light telling the hours. The woman writes,
her shoulders angled to the task.
One sheet of paper, all that is required.

Send for a new Vermeer to catch the silence,
the little window's light, my laptop's
scratched dull metal, the cheap pine desk,
the frame of the wheelchair, the carer beside me.
Watch as the distant leaves change bright for dim,
shadows relax on lawns, walkers on the unseen path
go home. Nothing amazes like the garden we have lost,
the naked baby before us, the severity of each moment,
errors folded, unfolded. The words not sent, not spoken.

Visitor

You bent down by my side,
leaned on the arm of the settee
where three of us sat. Three of fifteen
in the day lounge. You are most kind.
Got a dropped, half-chewed sweet
on your trousers to remember that.
Where I have ended up.
Days and nights lost at sea.

This is *Safehaven*
where the tides push us all.
We gasp on the dry land,
stagger up and down on it,
write messages in it for angels.
Wings outstretched, they can't stop now.

I am hankering after home,
slippery on the tongue,
I howl it like an abandoned dog: ho o ome.
Do you think I have become a child?
Some home, some dog's home,
the address keeps changing.
Am I a pup now? Are you my mother,
all teats, all tongue? But she would not be crying.

You look out of the window
for magpies or the undertaker,
something to amuse me.
Pass the parcel slowly till the claw
shows through to lift me to heaven.
You would like to believe it.

Every night I am kept here
you come and go, my flying island
that's you, and where do you go?
To my lawn's moss? To the outmost star?
Somehow you return. I think you
drive over a cliff somewhere, you land
in a flashing-blue-light box.
What do you come for? I am dying.
You can't croon me up from here,
I can't tail you out, my lyre-bird.
We know that, we don't like to mention.

I'm out in front on this one. Like a god
I put in meaning or extract it.
This habit of yours, this care for me
so old that it dies hard, what if you
cracked its case open and the wind blew?
What if it did not matter?

My cup spills over. Almost always.
Tea, soup, milk slops down chin, neck, shirt.
Full of days and their wide-eyed shadows.
What was hunger is my tray on time.
This thirst is baked on hell's hot cinders.
It would breathe fire if I had breath.

You've stopped trying the brightness.
I keep you waiting.
We'll be parted as soon as sorrow,
anything we say taken down,
useless, bent wheels dropped in the pit.

Save your vows for another day.
Let the waste in, let it trickle in
tendril by tendril, inquiring if
the space is available or might
be available, might it wait…
and tell it what I said.

Last words, soon enough forgot,
need strength I don't have.
No more flap out into air.
Hymn. Curtains. Off we go.
No applause in this case.

North Tees Epiphany

Up in the ship of warming air
I see earth roll, unroll ten miles or more
to the grey invisible sea, through terraces,
playgrounds, shops, car parks, wasted spaces.

The bridge an extinct spider, a clutch of long-
    cooled
towers, the low-lit clouds appalled
at the ruin of river, its nuclear cup
that must not be spilled, the whole brave balls-up.

This is where we live and if, we say if,
this airship, its skilful crew, deliver us safe
through the dream of our needful pain,
it's where we'll be glad to go home.

Always the engines' thrum as gulls weave
wind's fabric round and *Save us, save us*
their window-baffled, hardly-hoping call.
I am one ear of many, one eyeball.

Big ship's the grand, the theatrical show,
staging nativities three floors below
while this top deck sets tragicomic bones,
our breaks, distortions, fractures, agony.

Assorted healing heap, this ossuary soars
over the silenced houses, children, cars,
over the floodplain, over the ferny moor.
An hour to wait now for our visitors.

These faithful all will come, arise, adore
the new-born, the last-chancers, every floor,
will bring us frankincense and myrrh and gold
from down below, from out there's dark and cold.

Natural History

The dinosaur's all beams and rafters
in the bleached arch of its spine,
knotted and lumpy beyond ancient oak,
a bone-house baked in fossil stone.

And our two kids still arguing
all those years in the museum.
Could it be real? Was it a fake?
It is always time to go home.

My own backbone got no attention,
a lost relation of *triceratops*,
ghosting me, always a step behind,
shadow to standing starts and stops.

I dragged around this rucksack just in case,
a frame inside a flappy canvas skin
transported by the busy legs beneath,
an afterthought, I thought, of evolution.

Or it would bend to sky's unbending gaze
the ripple of a cyclist's bony spurs
in rainbow gortex visibility
between the saddle and the handlebars.

But over sixty years or so it seems
the weight of weight clamped in the vertical
squeezed disks together in a vice,
strangling the disregarded nerves' canal.

Now legs are left to dangle legless down
and struggle inching through each inch of plod,
the forward/backward/sideways shunts
my brain would manage if it only could.

The surgeons promise me that they will try
titanium. A rod or two might save
me from my frequent falls from grace,
redeem old fault lines from an early grave.

I hope they're right and, yes, I'll let you know
if they restore me to an upright stance,
swapping the dinosaur's demise
for leggy humankind's pretence.

Or kids can dispute if I'm fake or real,
the specimen that one day will be shown
in natural history's marble halls:
screwed space-age metal and primeval bone.

Flog It

Pack me down and out of
The Antiques Roadshow
to *Cash in the Cellar*:
experts, don't you worry,
shake your many heads:
'The key's condition, sorry, so
please wheel him off in his rusty barrow.'

And it's on a Sunday morning
at the Sellafield Bygones Fair,
on a fold-down operating table.
I'm a shivering junkie
in medias res, a brassed-off monkey
grinning like a Blair,
glowing in the rubble.

Bargain-hunter-gatherers,
faces like stale bread,
scuttle lithe as cockroaches
over the lino.
A fiver for me, a bite or a bean? No.
I'm nearly, almost,
might as well be, dead.

My minders won't enjoy this
jumble sale wail.
No room in the bin,
no hymn in the boot,
everything must go and make some loot.
The land is filled in
every leaky hole.

Away to the warehouse
of bankrupt stock,
flood-damaged Noah bathmats *et omnibus*.
It's warm enough and dry, they
won't kick up a fuss
if you leave them in the dark
and double-lock the lock.

Come back in the morning,
now the sale can start,
but you won't find me. Just
don't give a stuff,
a fart or a fistful of love. I'm off,
off to the incinerator
on a rare handcart.

Thank You, Jelly

I am making a hymn,
a praise song for this body,
which floats inert
down from my brain.

I want to thank it, this shivering blancmange,
this paralysed jellyfish, for all it has done
these past seventy years.
it has given my mouth so many meals,
it has shifted me over many miles,
it has made love for me, run itself out of breath,
it has undergone surgeries to keep me alive.
I cannot put a number on all its services.

Now it trembles at each whim
of the tide, alert to all sensation,
but has lost its sting.
Only my voice can shock you, electrify.
So I am helpless, but still
a trifle dangerous.

Housebound

You get a sense of what it's like to lie
alone and in the earth, set to decay.
The regulars will visit hallowed ground,
a few old friends include you in their rounds
from time to time, but most will let you rot,
forgetting they already have forgot.
Of course we can't know that for certain sure,
but some were coming and have missed the door,
while others phoned or emailed, sent a card
and, duty done, went shopping or abroad.
A few more didn't ask or realise
you'd disappeared from view. Whatever lies
beyond horizons can't be their concern,
they live for what's in range, don't seem to learn
what lurks outside their urn-shaped biscuit box
where sweets compacted lie, day's paradox:
it's not all-things, though beautiful and bright,
inevitably swallowed up by night.
Well, I might rattle on like this some time,
preferring home-grown groans to the sublime
of poetry, art, music, friendship, love.
Fact is, out there or, my conceit, above,
are many folk who care for me, who worry
about, pray for, want to help, will scurry
over if I call and ask. They'd lift me if they could
out of the grave, at least out of the mud
I have to blunder through just now. They can't
and that's the sod of what is most sincerely meant
but does not work, which makes me curse and
    blame

my well-wishers, for whom I'd do the same
if our roles were reversed, me up, them down.
Send them a card or flowers, a *Get Well Soon*.

Awake

The late-night film, old Bertolucci's *Dreamers*,
his only company, she as usual absent,
the cocktail of music, sex, cinema
nevertheless enough. He'll reinvent
what she told and might well not have told him
about the sixties, revolution, Paris,
lovers gone missing. From this merry mayhem
the long loop back to home and him she married.

Kept in that present like a dusty wreath,
he knows the argument still rakes her head
with how she could break out, might make the truth
just fit the day. *Dans la rue!* Knows how instead
she's grown slow compensations *sans merci*:
gardens, grandchildren. For better and for worse.

Easter in ICU

It is my body on this slab of bed
with one white sheet my cover.
No angels at my foot or head,
but nurses here, who hover:
they lift me, turn me over.

Their ritual attentions stalk
across this tomb, deep day, deep night.
My head rings with their echoed talk
of all that's wrong, should be put right.
I wish these suns were not so bright.

The surgeon has no plan to raise
me from the dead I imitate,
no flicker in his weary face
gives hope that I might levitate,
ascend to a more gracious state.

The nurses seek out breaks in skin
where bed-sore fiends can root and stretch,
while, like a roasting hog, my grin
turns on the spit, poor naked wretch.
Stripped bare, the bones are for the ditch.

Instead, let me be hoist aloft,
sole claimant to that bleak Cross Fell,
wind-broken bracken, peat sink-soft,
the weathershed of heaven and hell
where hikers' boots imprint like nails.

At the Window

Here I have watched
these trees grow large
and wide, the five
the space allowed,
that with each year
carry a greater weight
of branch and leaf,
blossom and fruit.

They make my plot content,
their unrelenting lack
of second thought
about expansion, height,
assuages growing pains.

Now in mid-May
they scatter drops of shade
over the mossy grass
that needs another cut
and over older man
who planted it and them
thirty-odd years ago.
He never dreamed
we'd still be here,
garden and gardener.

The children up and gone,
fencing renewed,
neighbours removed or died,
the most solid timber

split down with lightning,
which will strike again,
or storm or novel flood
sweep us to bonfires.

Today the earliest roses bud
beyond this window glass
the trees obscure.

The Leaving
for Julia

Taking my leave of you, the house, garden
where we grew three children,
was it that we had outstayed
our welcome or that, just tired,
this place needed a change of voices?

Though you had left some days before,
taken into care, which I could not provide.
Now my turn, the ambulance to a bare bed
and still more surgery. I never made it back
so you'd to stay away.
The house was emptied, up for sale,
our children's labours.
Trees lopped, hedging sheared, heating turned
    down low.

And all that said, four seasons
have gone their way,
my sense of sky's become
the emulsioned white of ceiling,
of sun, the ornate hung circle
of a shaded bulb,
my garden is cut flowers in water.

Winter hardened everything, hawthorn and
    pyracantha
lost berries, all bare sticks, sharp scratches.
By the garden window, that first green thrust,
tight fist of snowdrops bides its time,

will soon enough surprise new watchers
with its hard, pale pearls.

One day I came to see you, my wheelchair
strapped in the minibus, nurse by my side.
they placed us wheel by wheel,
steady as Moore's king and queen
on their Scottish hillside. We stayed two minutes
till my breathing blocked and I was rushed
to the hospital, leaving you bereft.
It was a tearing apart,
the last leaf sucked from the wood,
ripping its fingernails.

And now there are new owners,
making the house their own.
Peter from next door telling me this,
first project, a room for their one-year-old.
I think they will clear the garden
for the child's first steps,
for balls to roll and bounce.

Under the grass, weak as worm castings,
our weary archaeology, the bones of buried animals:
one pheasant hit on the Sunday morning run
to the swimming pool; one rabbit banned from
    your school
which would not dig its way out again.
Also, the procession of cats stalking through
    childhoods.

So next your turn to visit me,
our daughter driving, your carer by your side.
We did some talking this time, but dear me,
your anxious mind began its litany
of questions: is it time to go now?
And repetitions, till we set you free
to make your safe way home,
yet it was not your home.

Here, in the early hours
I often wake, hear the comfort,
your regular breath beside me.
But this is a single bed
and the breath I hear is the ventilator
filling and emptying my lungs.

Libby

at 12 weeks old

It's you up there, examines my old face,
spies something you can catch,
glimmers in the dark down here.
You cast a line of sensibility
which lures me, reels me in.
I watch your ancient, oceanic grin
shape for me, toothless and rounded.

Before you slip away, little fish,
dance of your fish-bright eyes,
sing me that song again:
ah…ah…ah…mm.
Fish, dolphin, mermaid, whale,
the music's baffling, beautiful.
In at the deep beginning, here
I learn to swim, love you for it.
We are in our element.

Promenade

after Horace

Now all you girls who kissed me when a lad
are like me, pensioned off, your time's been had,
and, if we met, we wouldn't recognise
each other's bodies, faces, years' disguise.
We'd walk right past the lips, the looks, the limbs
we'd dream about while singing the same hymns,
be put off scent by tweed coat, sheepskin mitts,
and not sniff out the perfumed smelly bits
incarcerated in hot nylon mesh,
be comforted by well-known spreading flesh.
My creaking sweethearts, you could teach some charm
to half-dressed totty tottering through Yarm
as if the cattle-market still existed.
I still admire the kind way you resisted
us clumsy boys' testosteronic gropes,
your patience as you taught us stronger ropes
of human love seeking a lifelong mate:
you knew that flowers had a fade-by date.
But did you find him you were looking for
or have you squandered sex on some dull bore
instead of chancing one wild fling with me?
Just think about it, as you make his tea.

Glazebury Girl

for Mary

Dark nights,
I met you on the steps down from The Tech,
your night-school class. From here
slow to the bus station,
last one for your journey home.
We dragged along the cindered backs
of Railway Road, pressing our weight
on damp yard walls, dank gates.
Under your watch-bright eyes
I learned the give and the resist
of lips, kissed, kissing,
while untaught hands quite failed
to make their way inside your winter coat,
its fingered tufts and curls of bluey-grey.

Summer was different,
gave no hour to hide.
We traipsed the pavements
by the East Lancs Road
or trailed the edges of flat, stubbly fields
which spread out from the village-string
of houses, farms, your chapel and the church,
dark stone against your family's cottage,
old apple trees shading your garden.

Invited there for solid Sunday teas,
triggering my dad's repeated joke
about your place: did you have
apple pie sandwiches? I never did,
that awkward, Brylcreemed lad,

soon to go off to university,
you'd taken up with at a Social
with Buffet or a Pie and Peas,
some chapel in the Circuit raising funds.

Those two young Methodists
all arms and legs, remembering each dance
learned painfully and now required.
First words exchanged, first glances held,
while cautious purses kept their change
for soft drinks and the bus fares home.

And what's become of them, of us,
it's hard to say, hard to write down
as fifty years and some have scratched
and scraped this page of mine.
What I have gleaned is this:
we are both still alive, but are grown separate,
as bolder loves and life-meant marriages,
as children's births and parents' deaths,
as faith kept seasonal through all the years
with ploughshare, seed-cast, reap and store,
or slowly set aside, all bramble-snagged,
have us quite prised apart,
unnoticed as the deep tectonic plates
nudging these northern plains and Pennine hills.

But I would like to know,
when all I know will soon be ignorance,
whether you still put trust
in that belief we shared in Harvest Home
before we had to reckon with
what all our days have brought us.

Perhaps God knows I tried, but years
wore down, wore through, the fabric tore.
At the back-end, I can't accept one Word
Incarnate, even as my flesh fails.
I might require salvation, but it wouldn't work,
cliff-hanger snatch out of the fiery pit,
Hell's teeth, jaws I don't think exist.

Back then, back there, we were child soldiers,
sunbeams in smoky air that Jesus wanted.
Polished and drilled in Sunday School,
knowing those hymns by heart,
we marched, we shone,
paraded our new clothes, bright as the banners,
in step with hired brass bands from pits and factories,
those Whitsun Walks that haunt forgetful streets.

And all of that's as far away
as you are now from me. I'm left
with distance and small mercies,
whoever gives, however given,
that I still count like blessings:
grandchildren's kisses, glimpses of poems,
the studied breath of the ventilator,
light through the curtains, learning to be content
with each day's mortal measure.

If you have stayed God-fearing, which I guess,
and full of expectation for the life to come,
I'll pray, for once, you'll share it with your own
    good sort,
kind Glazebury Methodists who make no fuss,
and not with clumsy-clever-clogs like me.

I really was one then, lacking the grace
to thank you for the love you showed
my dad, crippled, stuck in the Infirmary.
He kept on telling me how good you were,
lovely, but I kept sullen silence.
You and me, we'd finished, hadn't we?
And off I went again that hundred miles or more
up hill and down and far away to bury
head in books, mind in all those words.

So here I sit, have little left to say,
locked in this wheelchair's pew-hard seat.
Too many years gone, I can't face you now.
More miles, more hills than I will ever make.

From Cross Fell

Hardly the roof of the world
scraping at sky that thin.
More of a lean of leaky sheds,
a grey-green tarpaulin
hauled over, weighted down.

Water in flashes. Walls of stone.
The broken drainpipe path
up to this guttery ridge
can hatch out little eggs of blood
with grasses' wiry scratch.

From here down rain makes tracks
to seas each hand can reach:
close Eden's swampy tribe,
Tees by its high-dive foss,
the eely strands of Tyne.

Their floodlights fatten up,
fill in the long yards' cracks.

Long Meg

A campervan by the prehistoric stones:
dusk already, glad to be out of the field
and through the gate, I know the metalled road
from here to home but, still to be passed through
as I come nearer, the boulders in the ring
thicken like knots, make a noose round me.

Last of the sun backlights Blencathra,
great stranded whale on that luminous shore,
when I see the woman pacing and talking.
She shudders as I call across. The tall stone
and old oaks reach out fingers of darkness.
She wants to camp, the sign says No Camping.

She's dented the van's rear wing. On that low stone.
Reversing. Just when she needs to sell it.
Time she was back down under. For the hip op.
The van's not damaged much, fit for the breaker's.
I tell her there's a campsite three miles off;
she will not, she says, use campsites, needs nothing.

Or she could try at Melmerby, the green
travellers use after the Fair, she'd be fine
and the pub has good food. You go this way.
She will see. Don't leave it long, I say, night falls
faster now, sense it falling behind me.
Time I was away. I walk my last mile.

The road she should take. Cottage dark as walls
of a prison I taught in years ago,
been back in dreams inside. This night I've a key.

Nothing goes past my shadow down the lane.
Soon it's dawn, chaffies invent old curses,
do battle with the blue tits for the feeders.

I bike to the shop, bread and the paper,
the green's empty. Next to the daughters' circle
and the great stone chisel plunged into earth
where the light said to itself 'Stab, stab here!'
I see sheep in the ring, two crow-feathers
tied to swing from an oak.

Life Class
with a group of artists and writers

We are arranged, the four sides of a rectangle
its cracked edges these square work-tables
tops of scabby teak, others scuffed mustard.
Light is diffused through windows, higher cloud
sifting the rays, shadowing the bursts of rain.

Our model floats above the surface of floorboards
would polish back to oak, our model is laid out
on her lilo, old cushions from a lost settee
easy in private pool, the slightest breath
lifting her belly, fronds of her fingers stirring.
Dark weed hair falls into textures of cloth
clings in a moss where her legs part
from where they flow in their echoing lines.
The horizon of skull, the pencil stroke of eyebrow
the delicate fringe of one lid shivering
finer than any brush here, thinner than trembling
    lines.
The soul looks out, timid bright, from its hard shell.

Given how you lie and where I sit today
our model, your face is set away from me
in the gentle slope of a hill, its rise and fall
with, where men took stone, the flickering tarn of
    the eye.
And the wolds of your body slope up and away
not an abruptness, the angles camera might
    configure,
nor the abstractions of clothing. It is not

as an ideal either you are come here, but one
holding-together, while the glue's strong, the
    human genome
in a warming of sun, a conspiring of waters,
afternoon in the studio, from the life everlasting.

Along four edges, on the worn tiles of the tables
the writers bend to their ant trails crossing, re-
    crossing,
the artists intent on the scrape cries of charcoal.
Their creatures spring from your body and at once
are changing as you are, your indecipherable
nanosecond modulations, the reality of image,
the accretion of lines, the gathering of shadows,
our hands winding the sun through the sky
into a final darkness where, this same afternoon,
in mortuaries, quick dug graves, bulldozed in-fills,
the murdered lie unpuzzled under dry heaven.

Gentle-voiced man on his bed, one leg a pointing
    stump,
told me through camera and translator
'Bombs are not simple.' An expert followed with
the cluster's artistry, the swarms of copper bees.
They are too many to count, the war is over
as a heavy shower rattles the studio window,
simple enough, adjusts the wash of light
on your ribs and thigh, unwounded, whole,
our model. You after all may be
impossible, hologram of the maker's intention.
Young as you are, how else survived unscathed?

Design, target, trajectory: elements of purpose
exact as choice of brush, plain as one just word.
Galleries where time's to kill. I was never here
before, the poolside of your nakedness
our model. I am getting a glimmer of
this obstinacy of eyes and fingers,
their marks on paper, what they will lift from you.
Some understanding how we are small,
ephemeral, wavering in the light, plain lovely,
how we might celebrate earth made flesh
while we are.

Identifications

Hamstead Colliery, March 1908

Which were brought out of the pit.

Eleven lying in a group in three rows
on their faces, side by side
one on top of the road
one on Wednesday near no.19 cross road
two on Friday in no.1 east road
next day another, one more on Sunday
the last the Friday following

John Jones, collier – Ernest, younger brother
recognised the features
Thomas Summerfield – his three sons
Charles by his boots, John by his clogs, Walter by
    his shirt
Reuben Burton – his son, Enoch
by the description of his flannel band
also George Warner, collier – Enoch Burton
his flannel belt, his baldness
Wilfred Lawley – his brother, William
by his widow's (very ill, suffering now from fits)
description of his clothing
unable to recognise the features
Sophia Mitchell – husband, Samuel
his pipe, his knife, various articles
Fanny Bradley, widow of James
by means of his watch and chain and his bottle
Mrs Hancock, widow of James, last to be recovered
by means of a piece of cloth and a sock

Mrs Jones, Canal Road – twice married
her first husband
killed in the pit eleven years ago
four children by her second
their ages 6, 4, 3 and 2
him crippled in the pit two years ago
will never work again –
has lost her son, Joseph, breadwinner
the girl, 11, is crippled
the girl of 4 has a wasted leg
the girl of 3 has deformed limbs

verdict returned of 'accidental death'

Hydroponic

after D.H. Lawrence

Figs grow, ripen in Middlesbrough.
After six thousand years, by bold
strategic thinking, delicate
negotiations, a robust partnership
of key sub-regional agencies
here they are in Nature's World
palace of concrete and polythene
behind the Blue Bell in the bushes
these swollen dusty beetroots
these stallion's testicles gone rusty
these well-hung wonders of the hydroponicum.

Little wonder *Mother-in-Law's Tongue*
has ceased its wagging, gone green
or that a *Cup of Gold Wine* has
spilled down the wall of the hothouse.
Already there are reports of
giant plastic ladybirds
screwed onto tree stumps
where lanky whips of freckled stem
can have their way with them.
The exhibitionists of the plant world
are gathering, rubbery, tattooed intimates
flaunting blossoms like open wounds
pistils of pinky yellow.

Small Eden, free from soil, from weeds,
disease, from all imputation
sheltered from stormy blast, always in the light

temptingly fragile, easily seduced
when poets get their teeth into your figs.

Send for Zero, Hero and Nero
the intolerant ones
send for the Hydroporn Squad
the rays of flashing lights
the superintendent angel. Let them cast out
the grubby-fingered peddlers of verse
on the winds of dispersal, the muddy verges
of dual carriageways. Set up a working party
Figs in the Post-Industrial Economy
while there is still time
and issue protective clothing
to search school book-rooms
for hidden sunburst rhymes.

Horse-on-Tees

Thornaby's giant gull
and Preston's champion crow
hop and swoop,
eye up a Romany horse.

Shaky in the legs,
this Romany horse
and long in tooth,
been chipping away
at this mixed grazing
a hundred years,
fields of crazy concrete,
pastured paving.

Thinking of lying down
on what's left of them fields
and trying on dead for size?
A big mistake to make,
you tired old scrag-end.
No way these birds will consider you
art in a public space,
memorial to your lost race,
heroic licker up of polluted verges.

Meat is what they keep
in their cold stare,
eyeballing both your eyeballs.

After fighting talk, a little booze
and on-the-side
schmoozing beak to beak
with god-knows-who's,
they'd settle on one each,
throw a party after
in a convenient hostelry
with diner, mebbes the Eagle,
for senior associates, partners,
a greasy lawyer to chew.

Better for the rest of us if you
stay weary on your hooves at grass,
let another century pass,
see what the wind blows down
or the Tees shrugs out, what's
cooking on the gas turbines,
when the fair's in town,
who's sorry now.
And your bones won't get
planning permission,
not on this estate,
not on these well-lit roads –
the Council have made that
clear as their Crystal Mark.
Plain as a prairie.

Boro Fan

for John Duncan

My friend John's
a Boro fan,
supports the Boro
rain or shine,
win or lose.
He says
someone has to.

It's how you tell
a real supporter.
He'll be there, will John,
fair games, fouls,
good days, bad ones.
He says
someone has to.

Every season
these new signings
with wages bigger
than anyone dreamed of
when John was a boy,
they don't suffer.
He says
someone has to.

Most of them leave,
they get injured, they don't
come back from holidays,
their wives complain,

it's too cold, boring,
they catch the plane, John knows
most of them don't last.
He says
someone has to.

John agrees with them,
it's cold and boring.
They're right, not wrong,
they don't belong,
don't know the song,
haven't put the years in
on the terraces
the thick and thin years.
He says
someone has to.

It's John. He has to.
It's a job for life
being a Boro fan.
He tells me again,
he says
someone has to.

Over the Border

I'm looking for the Customs House
the old one, the way we were
before the transformation.

The river's invisible, licks
along down there, hums its burden
under crane feet, abstractions of the cranium,
glass-and-chrome emporia, o my *Boro Nova*,
an old cat sniffing out to the North Sea,
an old-fashioned stink to it.

Still looking for it, are you, the old one, the
    Customs House?
It isn't the Riverside, the stadium, all girder legs in
    a can-can?
Not the Transporter where the cars fly slow,
    traditional like
cargoes of iron ore, dogs' breath, slave-sweat, Serb
    girls, soft drugs, hard core?
Are you late for a meeting?

He doesn't know it, the Customs House,
he's new like the rest of us,
attacks the taxi he's repairing with a very large
    hammer,
doesn't know where it or Middlesbrough
or England is, only works here over the border,
    made it
to a street of car parts, brick caverns, spare dogs.
    In a white van

two men open their windows waiting for the boatman
who hasn't a clue, might have gone anywhere, if you
enquire at the metal box there, the window, the sign
    on the door.
                    – SECURITASK–

Trail two left legs through puddles, over rust heaps,
by old tyres, could have laid me down, could have
    cried
my one life, you don't need to read
The Cut-and-Paste Land, the bits you need on a
    shore are
the ruins, the illegal, the guard dog, the lingo, the
    raw stuff, the rusty sex,
the trespass, the trespass, the forgive us
who are late for our meeting, forgive us.

Oh has it a tower to poke at the clouds, to video the
    visitors?
You can't see it from here, like.

Metal sheet doorways, plastic blind window shields,
green flickering laughter of mudland where *ex
    cathedral* stood.
                    – RCIP–

Press the empty button, the enter yard, the gate
    says, the voice slides
and trips out the Customs House, the old one, the
    Excise, the Excuse,
the Hack Me Out, the Stab Me In, the new land you
    found it
all the lines cleared to the drop off the flat world.

Edwin Raymond, Music Maker

Aus Berlin, nicht wahr? But we never heard
that first language. When you left and found this
refuge, this new land, a second *Sprache*
you spoke with mastered emphasis.

You gave a rich return, your flute of flesh,
your spirit's strings, spelled out our shared birthright,
air, light and wings. You turned
our ears to touch, our lips to sight.

So you transformed each changing gummy label
for shifting-sand bureaucracies
to choirs and orchestras,
string quartets, symphonies.

Who will remember you, plain-suited hero?
In Stockton's church your name's engraved in brass,
your song in youth's cascading generations:
Freiheit, Endeavour, the Tees between its gares.

To Geoffrey Sheard, September 2007

I need a bridge through the shifting air
to reach from me to where this arch
of line and colour ends, wherever you are now,
a bridge of sighs, regrets, last words
we never spoke, broken-off projects,
all the stuff that kept us animated when we met,
that keeps me now in this one-sided argument.
You said I had the words in our debates on life and
    love,
on art and poetry. I use them now, all feathery with
    breath,
to reach you, if you hear me, with your praise.

Artist and teacher, which do I put first?
Each primed the other, slaked and stoked the other's
thirst, and such a trust between them they'd attack –
and no holds barred – with question, challenge,
    curiosity,
find satisfaction in this duel – duet – duality of
    learning.
There go those words again. You taught me reverence,
to see in a young child's marks on paper
the silent burst of understanding, the creator's joy
in this found world. And you showed me
your own marks on paper, how you strived
to catch that world in your net of skill and set it
free, set your soul free with it. By my bed
your 'Life Tree' 1978. I wake to it
over the radio chatter of the day and always sense
the universals and the urgency

that pulled the trembling wires of brain, eye, hand,
so often leaving you exhausted and unsatisfied.
While I and others looked on and admired,
you would be off again to find the lost
first makings of the life of earth, the stir
of spirit over the waters, the covenant
of rainbow.

Geoff, before you laugh
and knock me off this cloud of poetry
with some traditional West Riding quip,
it is time I stopped, waved you on your way.
So much I have not touched on.
Let all who knew you have their say, who loved you,
listen to them too. With me, as usual, all words,
shake hands, have a warm hug.
I'll try to say less, see more, learn a little.
At your end of the bridge, leave me a sign,
visual, strong, silent. Meet you in the snug.

For CAK, July 2008

After that last easing out of breath
happened – you weren't wary of it
and I was just a one hour visitor –
I thought so little about it, this was
after all the end. We close a book
expect no addendum or sequel, it's
too soon to talk about, give a view,
ascribe significance, a long story as
stories go and we got to the last word.
Your face was a woodcut, line and shade,
not a glimpse of fear or victory, just
the dim glitter of ice as you went cold.

Now days have passed with their decencies
you might join those minders in my head
I still make calls to. None that says much
even in dreams, hang around like
old coats by the door, coats of arms
in a dust-locked castle. Try to remember
the phrase, the particular photo, I can
rub, it stays on the page, doesn't light up.
Yet these, with a touch, a weary smile,
wind me to a good day I'll enjoy
different from first time. Can't be sure,
but expect you with a bag of embroidery.

What stories you might rehearse between
my ears. Will it be the same cast of builders,
taciturn men of the moor, children
of old friends who I know and have never met?

And might you complain you have nothing to read,
give your views on the state of the schools?
Thread through needle tellings, still if they're
gladdened by young hopes, reasoned faith,
sorting of strands in freedom's tangle... while out
    there
the family you drew close-stitched together,
strong-willed, generous, artful, with humbling love,
nurtures your sampler tree, inscribes your long,
    wise book.

The Shed Door

in memoriam John Savage, 4 February 2007

Early tomorrow in fog and frost
I'll hammer into shed's creaky door
one nail, not tried before, not touched with rust,
from the nail tin in the kitchen drawer.

One nail and enough to remember you with
who sank this morning into the grain,
one and a few heavy blows, as breath
left you the last time. Heavy as iron.

Many a time when I pass the shed
I finger those nails, by smooth and by rough,
know and think over the friends who have died.
The hammerer chooses us all soon enough.

Your nail will join them: straight, strong, bright,
telling the timber, while timber lasts,
you proved your metal under hammer's weight.
Early tomorrow then, fog and frost.

The Light

rubbing our tired eyes
the light
diving from the board the slow dive
the light
abseiling the sky
the light
writing its next-to-last will
the light
rendering the hills in its wash
the light
considering moonlighting
the light
speechless at what it signifies
the light
failing for everything
the light
wanting a bed for the night
the light
about to deny its name
the light
not comprehended after all that
the light
diminuendo
the light
reduced to a rim, pinned into stars, satellites
the light
bursting in horizon bubbles
the light
aquamarine, turquoise, emerald, bruising indigo
the light

going under for the third time
the light
    asking for a light
the light
    the black page spilling on its words
the light
    from all ill dreams defend our
the light
    leaving for home, leaving home
the light
    roosting in a wing-dark tree
the light
    the hiss of its first day fading and still
the light
    entering the tomb and counting to
the light
    turning perpetual morning

Down

Only the last of the light in puddles,
in wet eyes. Bullocks at metal gates.

The sky's a rush of tattered suits,
gabardines of grey, charcoal, ebony.

Over there America, little silver arrows
pointing the clear nights this way.

Bruises across a dark wall,
brambles with blue-black fruit.

I know to avoid barbed wire,
the sludgy trench, the night challenges.

Then road rolls out these children:
down they come in this mass trespass.

Uninvited they lift to scrutiny
every bright, brittle word I spoke.

Go back, the way I've come,
I sense the village like a face I've kissed

over and over. All its windows closed.
All its bodies alive and asleep.

Rain Falling

From the broken spine, the weary, worked-out hills,
my arm reaches to the trampled horizon,
    unravelling the dale,
thirsting in all its veins, stretched to that hand
    nailed to the gares,
the towering cranes, ships loading steel, the seals
    waiting tide's turn.

Down from this altar, cloud-wrapt source,
    inexhaustible weeping fell,
the sacrament of red clay flows, the anthem of
    gathering waters,
the heavens' fractured glass, bruising pools under
    high foss,
the draining of fields, settlements, factories. The
    bright cup of the sea.

Into the air, launch into the air, buzzard attending
    the rough high grasses,
heron spanning the quiet stretches, cormorant
    scouring the estuary,
hungry for the shiver of movement, the sliver of wet
    lightning.
My bones and flesh given to their tongues of flame.

Through this high window a distant line of greening
    trees shades in
my calendar, warmer spring, the wettest summer,
    my slow hours
grandchildren's birthdays dance through; we rejoice
    together,

their growing limbs, their love in learning life.
 May it last forever.

Rain falling to earth, its miracle, its succession of
 miracles.
A vision we can't comprehend, lacking the
 languages:
river music, birds of air, fish, seal flesh caressed by
 dark waters.
Be silent, listen. It is all of us, living and dying.

Spades

The king of spades
looks down on a golden table,
it's his. Everything is, he eyes
his shining reflection
in the golden table, admires
his ermined and embroidered belly,
his short sword, flat and edge
held up and down, his hard and golden hat.

This king has never held a spade,
hasn't driven it down in soil,
his hands are white, his furs are white,
he's never had to scrub
the dirt out of his nails,
delicate oval pearls, slivers of moon.

If he has legs, we aren't allowed
to see them. Feet and private jet
never touch soil. Where did
his fine fibres root, the sheep of his woollens
graze? Where did the winter stoat drag
its belly down to a hard stone, attentive
to prey? Or his hairdresser dispose
trimmings of royal beard?

When his flesh decays, it will be locked in stone,
in gold, in lead, in cedarwood, in silk.
Unsoiled, a proper worm-riddle.
Rich dead bones, safe as a saint's
in jewelled reliquaries, set into altars,

marbled in basilicas the tourists
wash through, tired of treasuries,
weary of granite floors and bright mosaics.

Look at us all, outside and afterwards,
bottoms on palace lawns, shoes off,
toes scratching at crusty clay.
We are sick of your majesty,
all your angelic orders.
We will queue at the ironmongers
again and again, the smell of soil
in our lost souls, the desire for our
garden back, our equality of earth.
We will return without passports,
carrying spades.

Advent

Now I am the Bishop of Somewhere
– some way off and not too important –
but live here with dogs and horses
and folk who know what life is about.
I wear loud sweaters and bark urbanely,
trot round the neighbours' houses
drinking their wine by night. Good to know
that geese still get fat, are even organic
and Christmas is coming with thank God no
    likelihood
of martyrdoms or pogroms but mince pies and holly
and pedigree conversation in Little Sodden
through which the Roman legions marched,
no angels under the standards of Constantine.

A Picture of March
for the children of Dunblane

Death and the resurrection
will stage the annual show,
massed bands of daffodils,
for the week-end holiday.
> *The blue sea spills*
> *from a broken cry.*

Spring will puzzle the crowds,
juggling miracles, see!
Eggs, rabbits, a sequinned god
sawn in half, and then!
> *The red sun burns*
> *and the knots untie.*

The river will crack the pastures,
a silver whip licking on clay.
The cows parade, abstract canvas
clowns swaying, spraying the ring.
> *The grey mist binds*
> *the wounded sky.*

Everybody will be up there,
prize-winners, hosanna-spenders.
Love will be led out, dance, enjoy
the food and drink of paradise park.
> *The green field dreams*
> *our dreams will die.*

The pageant, having its yearly turn,
passes, leaves only rinds, dried seeds,
the wrappers, rubbers, numbers
from the stained-glass machines.
The white flower bends
when you ask it why.

Where is the need to break open
bad news, in such plain colouring?
A most sharp loss, so young, lost here
where living is full of future play.
The painting-box is closed
in which the child must lie.

Legacy

To the young men – who all on earth are blowing it
in cars, on bikes, in minibuses, tanks and helicopters
et cetera, you young exploding over one hot planet
care of wheels and tracks, under wings or rotors,
blowing your thoughts and beliefs out, your fertile
    seeds,
prayer books and hymn sheets and political posters
that lift and drop their feathers of fireweed,
the dust into the dust into the dust –

I leave: my delight in autumn sweeping this
    churchyard;
a weather-wormed cross, sandstone, sharp by it
bright flowers all grief; words that double the doubt;
each child of mine and each child's child;
words that breathe and outdance me in the warmed
    air;
the blood's habit surging my heart there and there.

Turbines

When all our kind are gone
from what's then nameless earth
the storms will churn their arms
in this deep-fettered jive.

They'll grind on, celebrate
that they're God's children:
turbines and leggy pylons
in a conga of wiry limbs.

What questions they might ask,
find doubting answers to:
does the wind drive the song?
the song urge on the wind?

And what they are here for
after that fire, that flood,
where they are meant to go,
if there's a better place.

But we won't tell them,
won't care or want to know.
We have set them to dance
a last fling as the juice runs out.

The State of Play

Not much happens
in the state of play,
nothing important anyway.

The end is near
and it's time to start
so here we go on the stroke of the heart.

Nothing matters more
than the team we choose,
the strip we wear, the reds, whites, blues.

It doesn't last long
till the whistle blows
and the final score is nobody knows.

The sun's in the sky,
the sky's in the sea
and the seasons swing on the floodlights' tree.

Who goes up
and who comes down
dances the edge of a spinning coin.

The time of our lives
runs out to a cheer,
the crowds crowd in and nobody's there.

Today is the day,
it's here to stay.
Tomorrow and tomorrow, it's the state of play.

Near Midnight

Another day that sets out early summer,
its blossom and its warm air's flow,
what we all wish for when the times allow.

Which might be paradise, life's lasting version,
a rich stew (venison?) that extends
the senses past what doctors recommend

for our late years, steadily losing sap,
leaves, already limping along,
old dears sniffed out by dogs' hungers.

But days split more young brains and hearts
than they spill seconds. Pitiless
as those who lead us in our flashbulb blindness.

Listen, we won't hear tonight's music of
bereaved planets, dumb moons in cages,
comets tearing hair. See, nothing assuages.

There is no better day to die on, so much
unfinished, our solidarity with the snuffed-out
long resisted, though we read round about

despair, the unforgivable indulgence still
with no heaven to lose. The hapless universe
wants me as much as roses, foxgloves, cow parsley

which mint its thinginess in re-inventing selves.
Oh I will sleep, being midnight or almost. There's
hope my heart still pumps come morning's tears.

The Sands of Respite

Washed up that shore, we'd want to cling on there
however loud we claimed the opposite
nodding assent to all that urged us bear
the years' accumulating freight
on frailer shoulders, legs held up with sticks
and frames, arm-crutches, painkillers.

At mealtimes we'd discuss the various kicks
delivered since we last had chance to ask
survivors how they were and if the tricks
the physio played on muscles meant their task
of dressing, standing, walking was achieved
or they'd been stranded in the usual fix.

Well, life was given to us to be lived
and after sleep there'd be a bright tomorrow,
if you believed what's said to be believed
by those that had escaped this vale of sorrow
and offered gratitude in verse as lame
as those they left behind, those just arrived.

Staff pinned such pink and flowery rhyme
to notice-boards. Each butterfly
was crucified, the therapeutic game
got played, 'I can't walk', 'Try',
and every fall adjusted sweepstake odds
on black eye, cracked rib, broken limb.

Not meant to linger there: the rods
and whips of optimism drove us home

fast as they could, the special squads
were more effective than they'd sometimes seem
and how the dark dream ambulance
purred up and down along our beach of beds.

Till then, without a second glance
at what the future tries to hold and drops,
we'd focus on the daily do's and don'ts,
the present tense that neither starts nor stops,
the short-lived safeties of intensive care,
wrecked fellowship on such gaunt islands.

October

Nights drawing in, our visitors all gone,
and half way round the earth it might be
dawn and spring. But set your face for winter,
the sharp-tongued matron marshalling the yards.

The garden tries it, every live frond fades
where autumn in obsequious uniform
attends to grey and drooping beds,
the dying, the asleep, dark-cheery evergreens.

I see what passes by this box, this window,
a golden leaf swung on one thread of web,
then swept away, the silent night patrols.
First light, a blackbird makes the sparrows jump.

Such details score the hours, invigilate
each waning minute of the year.
Across the wards the shrinking days
scuttle like chaplains between disbeliefs.

What have we done? the wasted roses ask,
their washed-out blossoms shivered in
this last warm westerly. My way
to figure fall, cased, cared for, behind glass.

Closing Down

The world is full of half price sofas,
the universe getting that way. Cliffs of fall,
each hue of leather, fabric of your choice.
Between these mindless mountains, little me
in my wheelchair, doing my little wheelies,
reverse and forward, left and right,
thick pile carpet snags me. Drags me deep,
there is no escape from the showroom monster,
the grinning of the grim, grime-gulping
Drac, which scythes as it bites as it sucks
dust, dead flies, dried blood up, lost screws,
all detritus up, horsehair, human skin flakes, split ends,
life on this planet as we know it is from afternoon TV,
when the programme's not available, when one last
    blip
and the screen's gone blank.

All of my days I have abhorred this Vacuum,
this cyclonic howling, this baskerville wail,
this ingestion of every other breath,
this repeated monotone of the Reaper's call.

Look, it's the last few days, never to be repeated,
the sale of the millennium, the century, the decade,
the week. We shall inherit the earth.
With nothing to pay until we are dead,
when the army of robotic sweepers removes all trace
of our ruins, our straw house.
And never a two-year interest-free tear
for the species we'd worked so hard for, saved so
    hard for.

I know, I know,
at the closing down of the sun, everything must go.
All of us caught, packed into bags, boxes,
white fish, cheap fireworks, shipped to another planet,
sprayed out like crummy birds' eyes, fingers,
squirting like Catherine wheels,
slithering like mice droppings,
like the souls of our most loyal customers
through ever colder galaxies.
But not yet, I pray you,
my land of lost contents, my lifetime bargains,
hide me in the shadow of your wings,
the detachable, dry-clean shrouds, let me be,
my pale skin, my scored face, my limp limbs, my
    cracked wheels,
let me have one more turn of the sun, one last chance,
never to be repeated.

Still Life, Autumnal

Once sent, my spaceship camera
circles that distant sphere,
recording each parched detail,
connected with my brainy lens
to zoom in, track across
what is more than abandonment.

All things here look dry
and delicate, sculptured
in what appear as husks
but might prove more resilient
than metals from earth's ores,
than its hardest stones

or are indeed dust waiting on
one touch of absent breath,
one probing fingertip remote
to just disintegrate,
to atomise, to sift
into the barren plain.

Clusters of radar-pods,
spiny deterrent seed-heads,
dropped, unexploded, fluted shells,
and on this dry sea-bed
mines with the stubby thumbs
of pine-coned forest floors.

A fine apprentice piece,
a deathly beauty quite

out of reach, as if the god,
no less, had demonstrated
how he'd learned his craft,
then jumped the universe

to perfect in our close whirl
of air and rock and fire and tree.
The darkening hemisphere
shreds its used leaves, the other half
mints bright new currency
to light his globe of tears.

Uncollected Poem

Sanctuary

Two bony, meccano birds
Each side of river,
Neck-deep in mud,
Love divided, it's
Drawn into a kiss.
So beak tips meet
And fuse. A symbol
Of their passion,
Flesh stripped,
Raw as iron,
They carry the weight,
The world's burden.
Both shiver
In the slight sway.
Their mutual bond.
Their belonging
At this crossing place,
Together.

Published in *Everything Flows*, ed. Andy Croft,
Middlesbrough Borough Council 2012 to celebrate the
Transporter Bridge's first 100 years.

New Uncollected Poems 2013

Totentanz

I can only dig so far: field labourers,
mill hands, servants, colliers.
Down below that they fade
into no names, invisibility
of toil, of famine, of poverty.
They were serfs, peasants, wage slaves.
No heroes. The planet spins.

Do yellowing bones still clutch
traces of DNA like an old tune
round and round in the head?
Do these spiral up in me?
If so, my connection's made
with register and census glimpses,
a few papers, family Bible,
some of their heart in there.
Infants who waltzed away
before they knew their names.

But this is not the book of the dead,
no gold leaf, no spices, no precious stones,
no feasting. Their after-life
a deep ditch, not Dante's,
paupers' graves in a crowded churchyard
in the slums they were born to.

Who owned the land they lie in?
Those who made the chronicles,

history books, T.V. documentaries?
Barons, queens, factory owners, all the rest,
these in their tombs and sepulchres
with the same orchestra,
the same Okey-Cokey.

My plan is to join with
the anonymous dead,
forgotten soon enough,
no memorial stones,
I've seen too many.
I will hold hands with death
and all of you, my folk,
in the glorious dance of the earth.
Nothing but earth.

Thunderflies

The garden is aswarm,
minute black flies.
At once they are on me,
in my ear, on my arm.
A tickling torment.
My carer has to remove each one,
"What are they called?"

Suddenly I remember: "Thunderflies."
Am working with John Peake
on Tommy's farm those teenage summers,
following the reaping machine,
it throws out bundles tied with loose string.
Stooking up, one from each side,
pushing the heads of the sheaves together.
Two times four, making a tent
for the air to blow through, dry the crop.
One day no air, but thunderflies.
We looked for the darkest cloud,
a flicker of lightning, anything to drown
them, get us under the hedge.
But no thunder. Just brooding stillness,
the flies in our eyes and hair.

Back home I wash in the sink,
pull dead flies from each eye-corner,
comb a mess of them
from sun-bleached hair.

No thunder in this quiet garden,
just the flies. Time to get out of the sun,
creak up the wheelchair ramp.
Those days are lost,
most of their people dead.
Inside, free of those harbingers,
wait for the god to strike.

Parental

When both of us are dead, you'll know
how bare your heads are to the sky,
and of those things we never told
well, any one of you might say,
if I had asked them this or that,
but too late now, the scent's gone cold.

As for your young misdeeds confessed
years afterwards, mischievousness
we never caught you at,
never thought you so bold,
well, let it go with breath
or if there's more to tell,
lay it, with us, to rest.

I, Said the Fly

All this last summer
you have suffered us
and wished us gone
from house and garden,
unable to lift a finger.
Bodies, you ought to know,
are painful. Now I am here
circling above your bed.
Hundreds of cells
in a convex curve: you exactly.

Aerial photography prepares the raid.
There is the white plain of your linen.
There is the outcrop of your head,
where I explore and satisfy
my curiosity. With my kith and kin,
all one, all angels, sculptors in flesh
remove the tyranny of pain,
discovering the blank ideal,
the anatomy of bone.
This is our daily bread,
our artistry and sustenance.

Now I taste your sweaty pores,
harvest the flakes of skin
among your head's sparse hairs.
I feel you thinking how the days diminish,
the rusting leaves spell autumn,
the end of our dominion.

Your relief will come with brief-sunned
winter hours in a shortening life.
We shall return, always,
the world requires us.

Notes to the poems and acknowledgements

November Photographs (Platform Poets, 1981)
Some of these poems first appeared in: *Phoenix,
Yorkshire Review, Behind the Lines, The Northern Drift,
Response, Those Who Can't Do, The Use of English*, and
Poems (Andrew Stibbs and Gordon Hodgeon) The
Haworth Press.

A Cold Spell (Mudfog Press, 1996)
Some of these poems have appeared previously in
the following magazines, programmes and
publications: *Behind the Lines, Continuum, The
Northern Drift, Phoenix, Poetry Durham, Response,
New Writing from the North, various Write Around
anthologies* (1989-1992). Thanks to those editors and
selectors.

P 85 Tractor and Plough is on a community
ceramic in the community hall in Hunsonby.

Winter Breaks (Smokestack Books, 2006)
Acknowledgements are due to the editors of the
following publications in which some of these
poems first appeared: *Kenaz, Penniless Press,* Cynthia
Fuller & Kevin Cadwallender (eds) *Smelter* (Mudfog
2003), Subhadassi (sel) *The sensitively thin bill of the
shag* (Biscuit, 2003), Maureen Almond (sel)
Challenges (Biscuit, 2005), Cynthia Fuller & Andy
Croft (eds) *North By North East* (Iron Press, 2006).
'The Price You Pay', then titled 'Cycling To The
Rainbow', won the first Mirehouse Poetry Prize,
Keswick, 2004.

Winter Breaks sequence:
Based around the twenty-four poems by Wilhelm Müller, which Franz Schubert took as the lyrics of his song cycle, *Winterreise*. Müller's anonymous wanderer is a young man rejected in love, an outcast tramping through winter landscapes which provide a plenitude of images to mirror his emotional and psychological states. The *Winter Breaks* isolate, also nameless, is much older. His winter, partly that of age, has its own contemporary qualities and is also informed by his familiarity with the Schubert songs and their young protagonist, whom he disparagingly calls Brokenheart. Other myths intrude and mingle in this older, later and more curmudgeonly (his word) head. Like Müller's 'Brokenheart', he converses with himself and at times addresses a lost or absent or distanced lover. The epigraphs are taken from the author's English versions of the German lyrics.

P 119 Tomb Decoration: Cattle - from the British Museum.

P 121 Song for Mario: written in response to the Michael Radford film *Il Postino*.

P 124 The Afternoon Slot: many Teesside writers benefited from creative writing courses held at Leeds University's Harrow Road Adult Education Centre in Middlesbrough through a large part of the twentieth century. The Centre, axed by the University a few years ago in order to cut spending on non-essentials like lifelong learning, has since shared the fate of much local industrial plant: demolition.

Still Life (Smokestack Books, 2012)

Acknowledgements are due to the editors of the following publications where some of these poems were first published: *English in Education*; Colette Bryce (ed) *Ink On Paper*; Andy Croft (ed) *Speaking English: Poems for John Lucas*; Richard Jemison (ed) *Teesway One Nine Nine*; Bob Beagrie and Andy Willoughby (eds) *The Wilds*. 'Over the Border' won the Mirehouse Poetry Prize, Keswick in 2007.

Gordon Hodgeon was born in Lancashire in 1941. He has worked in schools, in teacher-education and in various educational projects. From 1972 to 1996 he was a schools' adviser in Teesside, later Cleveland. He was active for many years in NATE, in Northern Arts, Cleveland Arts and New Writing North. For several years he ran Mudfog Press. His previous books include *November Photographs* (1981), *A Cold Spell* (1996), *Winter Breaks* (2006) and *Still Life* (2012). After spending the best part of four years in hospitals and rehab units, he now lives with his daughter and grandson in Stockton-on-Tees.